814.54 Fre
Freeman, Becky, 1959-
A view from the porch swing :
musings on a complicated search
for

34028053786423
ATA $12.99 ocm??903490

RECD MAR 3 0 2004

W9-DAG-225

3 4028 05378 6423

A VIEW *from the*
PORCH SWING

DISCARD

Presented To
Atascocita
Branch Library

Harris County
Public Library

By
Friends of the
Atascocita Library

DISCARD

A VIEW *from the* PORCH SWING

Musings on a complicated search for the simple life

BECKY FREEMAN

Best-selling author of *Worms in My Tea*

BROADMAN
&HOLMAN
PUBLISHERS

Nashville, Tennessee

© 1998
by Becky Freeman
All rights reserved
Printed in the United States of America

0-8054-6097-7

Published by Broadman & Holman Publishers, Nashville, Tennessee
Page Design: Anderson Thomas, Nashville, Tennessee
Editor: Vicki Crumpton
Typesetting: ComCom, R. R. Donnelly

Dewey Decimal Classification: 814.54
Subject Heading: HUMOR
Library of Congress Card Catalog Number: 97-39216

Unless otherwise stated, all Scripture citation is from the NIV, the Holy Bible, New International Version, copyright © 1973, 1978, 1984 by International Bible Society. Other versions cited are the New King James Version, copyright © 1979, 1980, 1982, Thomas Nelson, Inc., Publishers; KJV, the King James Version; *The Message*, the New Testament in Contemporary English, © 1993 by Eugene H. Peterson, published by NavPress, Colorado Springs, Colo.; TLB, The Living Bible, copyright © Tyndale House Publishers, Wheaton, Ill., 1971, used by permission; and NASB, the New American Standard Bible, © the Lockman Foundation, 1960, 1962, 1963, 1968, 1971, 1972, 1973, 1975, 1977, used by permission.

To send Becky a note or inquire about speaking engagements,
you may contact her via E-mail at beckyworms@compuserve.com

Library of Congress Cataloging-in-Publication Data
Freeman, Becky, 1959–
    View from a porch swing : musings on the complicated search for the simple life / Becky Freeman.
        p.   cm.
    ISBN 0-8054-6097-7 (trade paper)
    I. Title.
PN6162.F744   1998
814'.54—dc21   97-39216
                                                                                            CIP

1 2 3 4 5 02 01 00 99 98

In Loving Memory of Sam Meserve

He managed to make every baby he rocked feel secure,
every child he hugged feel ten feet tall,
every teenager he encouraged come away with new confidence.
He greeted every woman as if she were a princess,
every man—no matter his status or appearance—
as a friend and a brother.
We, who were privileged to know Sam,
couldn't help thinking,
My, how that servant takes after his Master.

Thank-yous to all who have shared my porch swing with me—

My sweet husband, Scott

My precious kiddos—Zach, Zeke, Rachel Praise, and Gabe

My incredible parents, George and Ruthie

My parents-in-love, Jim and Beverly

My crazy, wonderful siblings and other kinfolk

Dear friends and kind, country neighbors

The folks up in Nashville who help put me between these covers

You, my cheerleading readers,
whose "rah-rah" notes, E-mails, and prayers
keep me laughing and encouraged.
On those "uninspiring days," it is often *your* words
that give me courage to put *my* words on paper.

And finally,

Praises to the Creator of all—
for coming out to meet us
in porch swing moments.

table of CONTENTS

Table of Contents

TABLE OF CONTENTS

TABLE OF CONTENTS

introduction

I'm in love with porches: front, back, wraparound—you name it—they are my friends. Ditto for backyard decks and boat docks, treetops and river rocks. They're wonderful places to ponder or shell a peck of black-eyed peas. Great surroundings, these, to do what our grandmothers called "settin' a spell" or what we call "vegging out." But to me, the prime spot for "settin' and shellin' and mendin' " will always be the Great American Porch Swing.

As a matter of fact, when my mind was in dire need of some mending, I committed myself to the Institution. The Great American Porch Swing Institution, that is.

It all began about a year ago, on a day when my mother drove out for a visit to our country home. . . .

A View from the Porch Swing

The afternoon unfolded sun kissed and lazy. Since mother had retired from writing, we had no book business to discuss, no agenda planned out. For both of us, I think, it was remarkably fun to just hang out together on that autumn afternoon.

Observing my mother's tiny figure tucked neatly into her slim-fitting jeans, I thought, *I can't believe Mother's almost sixty—she's still so attractive and full of spunk.*

We sank onto my red plaid couch, each of us sipping at our warm mugs of tea, with me trying to arrange my legs in a way where my thighs wouldn't do that awful bulging thing they do when I sit down. I finally gave up and tried tugging my oversized flannel shirt over them instead.

"Becky, quit that," Mother said. "You look great. Relax." (Does anything escape a mother's notice?)

So I folded my legs up comfortably, ignoring the bulges. Then I really began to unwind, pouring out my thoughts of late—sharing from the secret corners of my mind, where Really Big Ideas seem to pool and mull. It was one of those times when I let my words flow unchecked, chaff and grain alike, like falling leaves on a velvet breeze. Mostly, I'd been pondering one simple question: *How can I live out the rest of my days with a greater sense of laid-back joy?* (As opposed to my accustomed high-gear stress.)

I was on a philosophical roll, a mental runaway train. When I finally paused to draw in breath, Mother gave a deliberate nod of her wise head.

"I know exactly what you mean," she said.

You do?

"You do?" my words echoed the thought. Perhaps I was not an alien life-form after all.

"Oh, yeah," Mother declared. Then she placed her cup on the coffee table, enabling her to gesture freely. "It's just like I felt the other day when I was watching an old rerun of *The Andy Griffith Show*. There was a scene where Barney and Andy were sitting on the front porch swing, chatting and chuckling and stopping here and there to sigh at the stars. Something inside of me leaped, and I thought to myself, 'We aren't doing enough sitting and swinging and shooting the breeze anymore.' "

"Mother! You are brilliant! That's it—I want to swing on the porch, glide back and forth in an easy rapport with my husband and kids and friends. I want to prop one leg up, lie back, look at the stars—and shoot the breeze with the One who made them. I want to slow down, simplify—be at home in my own head. What I need is a Mayberry of Soul!"

As part of my quest for a Mayberry Soul, I began taking thirty minutes to an hour, sometimes more, almost every morning to rock my soul in the bosom of our back-porch bench. Instead of dragging myself back to bed whenever I was hit with the blues, I came out swinging instead.

After a few weeks of this rocking ritual, I suddenly realized how much more joyful, refreshed, rested, and balanced I was beginning to feel. (Or as balanced as a woman "so right-brained she pulls to the right and walks in circles" can ever hope to be.) I was on a real upswing (pardon the pun), even thinking at times I might die from an overdose of contentment.

Sometime later, as I was reading in the Old Testament, I stumbled across an ancient God-given formula for maintaining the well-being of earth and its inhabitants. God told the Israelites to take a special Time-Out, an entire year in fact, for rest and refocusing (Lev. 25). Even the earth was to be left alone to sleep and renew itself. Suddenly, the reason I was experiencing a personal blooming of my own became clear. There's a certain type of replenishment needed for growth, and without realizing it consciously, I'd been taking in just the sort of steady nourishment my body, soul, and mind had been hungering for. Humans, like fertile soil, need regular times to lie fallow in order to recharge and function well.

As a transplanted country gal, I was also pleased to note that this Hebrew time-out ritual had a country-style, fun-to-say ring to its name. It was called the Year of Jubilee. Try saying *jubilee* three times without smiling. (Or without using an accent that sounds like a character from *Hee-Haw*.)

Every fall my hometown of Greenville, Texas, gears up for our annual Cotton Jubilee—a traditional celebration of our local fall harvest with junk food and foot-stomping music, folk dancing, and crafts. There's also the annual Downtown Bed Races: a race in which businesspeople push their company-sponsored beds-on-wheels—made up to look like parade floats—down Main Street. It's the hodgepodge, goofy-fun festival small towns embrace and perpetuate, a merry departure from the mundane.

And certainly, an annual event such as this is a partial fleshing-out of the term *jubilee*. But this joy-bursting word means so much more. It is one of the most liberating concepts I've happened upon in my life. It will take me a whole book to share it all. But as they say around these parts, "I'm itchin' to do it."

If you have a porch of any sort, you might want to take this book and wander outside to read it. If you have a porch swing and the day happens to be lovely, so much the better. If not, find another spot to call your own, take your shoes off, put up your feet, and get comfy and cozy, because I have a passel of stories to help you unwind—to help usher in a Personal Porch Swing Jubilee.

Ya'll, this is gonna be fun.

"Are you tired? Worn out? . . . Get away with me and you'll recover your life. I'll show you how to take a real rest. Walk with me and work with me—watch how I do it. Learn the unforced rhythms of grace. I won't lay anything heavy or ill-fitting on you. Keep company with me and you'll learn how to live freely and lightly."
(From Jesus' invitation, Matt. 11:29, *The Message*)

chapter one
COMPLICATING
THE SIMPLE LIFE

I am constantly amazed and amused by this life I'm now leading—
so far removed from the one I once knew.

The other day I drove to the high school with my thirteen-year-
old daughter, Rachel. I asked her to take a sports drink to her older
brother, Zeke, who was about to begin an after-school session of
football practice. She soon returned, breathlessly diving onto the
front seat.

"That was fast," I commented. "Did you give Zeke the
Gatorade?"

"No," she responded calmly. "I gave it to Goof."

"Pardon me?"

"I gave it to Goof Fry and told him to give it to Zeke."

"Hold it. Are you telling me there is a child who goes by the name of 'Goof' at your school."

"Yep. It's what everyone calls him."

"Even the teachers?"

"Mo-*ther*, yes! I said that's what *everyone* calls him. The teachers, his parents, the whole school. Nobody ever thinks about it being strange or anything. He's Ida Lou's brother."

"So, let me get this straight. There are a pair of siblings in your school named Goof and Ida Lou Fry."

"Yes."

I grinned. Rachel, eyeing me suspiciously, asked, "What are you smiling about?"

"Oh," I replied, "I just love country life, that's all."

On our way home, Rachel and I stopped at the local grocery store to pick up a couple of hot barbecue sandwiches and some cold Dr. Peppers. There on the counter was a flyer from the taxidermist next door. "This is too good," I said aloud as I scanned the paper. Here, in brief, are the contents of the flyer:

VARMINT TOURNAMENT
BOBCATS 100 POINTS, COYOTE 50 POINTS
BIG CAT AND BIG COYOTE
JUDGED BY WEIGHT, NOT BY LENGTH.
ALL ANIMALS ENTERED IN CONTEST WILL BE
CHECKED THOROUGHLY TO VERIFY FRESH KILLS.

LET'S KEEP THIS AN HONEST AND FUN EVENT.

How would one go about cheating in a varmint contest? I wondered. What? Do some unscrupulous hunters try to fluff up road-kill and pass it off as a freshly killed varmint?

I haven't always been surrounded by bobcats, coyotes, and roadkill—or people with names like Joe Bob, Linda Sue, Goof, and Ida Lou. I grew up in the suburbia of *The Wonder Years*—complete with cul-de-sac, Country Squire station wagon, copper-tone appliances, and a hot pink, orange-and-yellow-daisied bedroom. But even back in the groovy '60s and mod '70s, I longed for a simpler, country-style life. While my friends dreamed of being models in New York City, I pictured myself growing up to look like Mary Ann from *Gilligan's Island*. In my daydreams it was always a spring morning. I would be wearing a red-and-white gingham dress, singing as I fed the chickens in front of my farmhouse, which was surrounded by white picket fences, tweeting birds, and jersey cows lowing in the distance.

Though I did turn out to look somewhat like Mary Ann (only slightly more "well-rounded"), my favorite TV role model was actually blonde, pigtailed Ellie Mae Clampett from *The Beverly Hill-billies*. I thought she was one of the prettiest, sweetest girls on TV, and I determined to grow up to be just like her. (It never dawned on me that my heroine's IQ was just slightly below that of an average possum. Even more frightening, there was a period of time when I thought Jethro would have been quite the catch.)

By the time I was fourteen, I knew every one of the late John Denver's back-home-again songs by heart. (I must confess, I still do.) I especially liked the one about blowing up the TV and moving to the country and raising kids on peaches. Then I fell in love with Scott, who looked a lot like John Denver at the time: straight sandy bangs, square jaw, wide smile, and wire-rimmed glasses.

Though we lived in the burbs, my parents hung a rustic porch swing in the backyard where Scott and I did our share of old-fashioned courting. Much to my delight, I discovered during one of our snug chats that Scott shared my Picket Fence Dreams. When we married in our late teens, we could only afford a small duplex in town, but we spent many an evening planning the day when we'd break free from suburbia and head to the hills.

By the time our first two sons, Zach and Zeke, were born, we'd saved a little money (a whopping three-digit figure as I recall) towards making our dream a reality. We'd buckle the boys in their car seats and drive out of the city every chance we'd get in search of our own piece of down-home paradise. I even made up a little "lookin' for a home" ditty. The kids and I would sing it at the top of our lungs as we drove winding roads around herds of cattle and rolling green pastures.

> We wanna live way out in the counnnn-try
> Way out with the roosters and the frogs—
> We wanna live way out in the counnnn-try
> Way out with the milk cows and the hogs!

We finally found our spot—a one-acre wooded tract with a pond—about thirty miles from town. Investing our meager life's savings, we proceeded to make the first of our many hayseed dreams come true: We built our own log home. Not from one of those Lincoln Log Kits either; we built ours from *scratch*. Actually Scott did almost all the work. My contribution was mostly chasing kids and cheering him on. Besides, I was expanding again, or as Scott would put it, we had "two kids underfoot and one in the oven."

After graduating from college, Scott made a living as head of his own building company. Now he found himself specializing in log construction full-time. I doubt there was ever a job more suited to a man and vice versa. To go with his log-splitting career, Scott grew a full beard. His standard uniform became boots, jeans, and a flannel shirt—sometimes he even added red suspenders. My mother took to calling him "Dan'l" or "Abe."

For five years, Scott supervised and participated in the crafting of gorgeous homes and buildings out of logs—cedar, pine, and aspen wood—accented by hand-carved staircases, rock fireplaces, and custom designed woodwork and cabinetry. The downside of this particular dream-come-true was that we never got to keep any of the log homes he built; we had to keep selling them to keep the bills paid in his newborn business. I remember distinctly one eighteen-month period when we moved *five* times.

In short, the simple life we were creating was getting awfully complicated.

Then came the well. If you lived in the country and didn't have your own well, the neighbors across the pasture might think you were nothing but city-water-drinking sissies. Not one to let his family suffer shame, Scott proceeded to dig our own bona fide country well. To much fanfare, he and his buddies hauled in and hovered over the well-digging machine as if it were a goose about to lay the golden geyser—sure that any minute they'd hit "pay water." A week later, when the machine finally stopped somewhere near the earth's core, they hit genuine H_2O! There was whooping and hollering and all sorts of commotion going on—that is, until a rusty wrench accidentally slipped out of Scott's hand, disappearing down the world's longest pipe. It got so quiet you could have heard a pin—or in this case, a hand tool—drop.

We were finally the proud owners of our own well—complete with running water. However, the water that came out of our faucet was a deep shade of burnt orange. After bathing and washing all our laundry in our country-fresh well water, our family looked like a matched set of rusted tin men. At that point in our lives, we lived in a beautiful, two-story log home—but every morning we'd sheepishly walk over to the neighbor's to fill up canisters with decent drinking water. Our simple life had taken yet another complex twist.

Today, at last, we own another country home and, at this point, cannot imagine ever selling it. It's also on a wooded acre or so, near the edge of a small lake. It is peaceful, scenic, and serenely beautiful, though the last several years have been anything but simple. We, a family of six, started out in this particular spot in a one-bedroom, 850-square-foot cabin. Scott has now spent the better part of the last eight years—nearly every weekend—remodeling the cabin into a two-story house. (If you've read my other books, you've been following this house-raising saga for several years now.)

Zachary, our eldest, finally got his own bedroom. (He enjoyed it for all of three months before he graduated from high school, took off for a summer job in Indiana, then headed to college.) The long-awaited, much-anticipated second bathroom also arrived! (We held hands and had an emotional family celebration around the new commode.) However, I still have a full set of kitchen cabinets, three table saws, various stacks of lumber—and yes, probably a partridge in a pear tree—stacked on my front porch.

I'll admit, we are not your normal, everyday family. Even so, I don't think we are alone; few city dwellers fully realize what they are in for when they choose to "cash out to country" and dive into the simple life.

Lifelong residents here have names for us newly countrified folk: High-Rise Hillbillies, Bumpkin Boomers, Yokel Yuppies, and my personal favorite, Cappuccino Cowboys. Our family used to be the lone transplants out this way, but suburban refugees are popping up all over our neck of the woods now—each trying their best to homestead, unobtrusively, among the natives. Try as they might, it's impossible not to stand out. The other day—honest—I heard one of our Cappuccino Cowboys was out baling hay wearing a neatly pressed Oxford shirt and $250-dollar shoes, his Rolex watch glinting in the sun. In his defense, rumor has it he *was* wearing overalls and a cowboy hat at the time.

A couple of years ago, I overheard a conversation between a Lexus-driving, tennis-playing, recently transplanted female and a woman who's been "born and reared in these here parts." The local woman spoke first.

"So, Hon, you oughta come out with us tonight and go coon huntin'. Ain't nothin' more fun."

"Oh, really?" the newcomer replied, touching her manicured nails to her chin. "That sounds very interesting. And what exactly do you do with the little raccoons once you've found them?"

"Why, we eat 'em," came the matter-of-fact reply. It was like eavesdropping on Ellie Mae inviting Ivana Trump over for "a mess of grits and victuals."

Though we have no shortage of varmints and victuals, if there is a drawback to living in a small, rural town it's that we're hard up for exciting news. The police reports are on the order of, "Two sticks of gum found missing from local kindergarten teacher's desk. Suspects being held in the corner." Columnists, too, are scraping the bottom of the barrel to find interesting information to share in the local newspaper. I hold in my hand an actual clipping in which one local columnist informed the entire community that she's "been hacking up phlegm all morning." Now there's a lovely and newsworthy tidbit to digest with your morning coffee. Still, a lack of excitement is a small sacrifice for a peaceful life lived close to nature.

Even as I look back on the complicated road we took to get to this simple life, I have to smile and say it's been worth every rusty drop of water, every log we ever laid, every coon and possum we've had for supper. (No, not *eaten* for supper. But sometimes they do wander in from the woods for a dinnertime visit.) Why? A thousand reasons, but tonight I was given just one more perfect example.

This evening Scott was working late, and Zach took his brothers to the bowling alley. I asked my daughter, Rachel, if she'd like to join me for a bite to eat at Grant's Cafe. (Side note: We have very few stores in this area, but one is called Gantt's Village Market, the other is Grant's, with an *r*, Cafe. If you don't think *that* keeps us

Yokel Yuppies tongue-tied!) Anyway, by the time we finished our meal, I'd visited with two waitresses. (We all, of course, know each other by name.) I found out one had an awful sinus headache, and I offered her sympathy; the other had just won a free Caribbean vacation, and I offered her my jealousy. This doesn't even count the folks we greeted coming in and out of the restaurant during our meal.

At one point, a cowboy strode in the front door, making a public announcement to the entire restaurant: "It's comin' down a gully washer out there!" As he shook the water from the brim of his hat, his cafe audience responded with thoughtful comments: "Sure 'nuff is." "Heard the TV weatherman say there was gonna be a frog strangler a comin' in." "Yep—but I never put much stock in them ol' boys." "Looks like he was right this time, though, boy howdy. Listen to that thunder!" "Yep." "Uh-huh." "Yes, siree."

Rachel and I joined in the group conversation until we finished our meal, paid our check, waved good-bye to the small crowd, and ran through the rain to our car. After starting the engine, I pulled out of the drive. That's when I did what's affectionately known around here as, "a Becky." Somehow I managed to land the car nose down in a muddy ditch.

If I'd been in the city, I'd probably still be stuck, nose down in the mud, waiting on some tow truck, at fifty dollars an hour, to come haul me out of my dire predicament. But not in Small Town, U.S.A. Before I could roll my window down, I was surrounded by able-bodied men in boots and caps, concerned women and children, and assorted pickup trucks—all standing ready to lend aid and comfort. The owner of the restaurant, Mr. Grant himself, came out laughing, saying, "Becky, why am I not surprised?" and donated a new rope to the cause.

Within fifteen minutes, I'd met four new people and shared several laughs, wondering aloud if there was ever a ditch my hood hadn't met. One of the pickups beamed its headlights, while the other one yanked on my car's back end, and in no time I was un-stuck and on my way home. I don't have to depend on the kind-ness of strangers because no one's a stranger in small communi-ties like this. And isn't that, after all, what the simple life's about?

Now we live way out in the counnnn-try
Way out with the roosters and the frogs—
We live way out in the counnnn-try
Way out with the milk cows and the hogs!

Yeeeee-haw!

The LORD *preserveth the simple.*
(Ps. 116:6, KJV)

chapter two

CHUCKLING FROM THE HEAVENS

Even before we moved to the country, my life was weird. I continue to attract a steady stream of weird people and circumstances. Admittedly I am odd at times, but I'm about ready to accept this fate as my life's work and mission. Every so often someone will tell me, "Becky, God has His hand on your life." And I believe that to be true. But I don't think God's hand is on me the way it has been on great saints of the faith I've read about. More often I feel as though God's hand reaches down, here and there, giving me a playful poke in the ribs. Could my heavy purpose on this planet be simply to lighten things up?

About a month ago I decided to clean out my old station wagon (which we lovingly named Sag) before I darted into the local mall. I hurriedly stuffed trash from the floor and seats into a plastic bag. But somewhere between my car and the mall I must have gotten confused. I thought I had my purse hanging from my arm, when in reality I was dangling a lovely plastic bag of refuse. There I was roving the mall, conversing with salespeople, like one of those bag ladies we so often see caricatured in movies—the kind who honestly think they look quite sophisticated carrying a bag of trash filled with straws, paper cups, and half-eaten tacos, looped daintily over one arm.

More examples, you ask?

A couple of weeks ago I rented a car for the day to drive to Dallas. (Sag had a bad cough, and I was afraid he might catch the flu if I took him out for a long drive.) That evening, Scott planned to follow me in his truck back to the rental car facility so I could return the car. We walked out of the house together toward the driveway—Scott heading to his pickup, me to the rental car. But as I tried to open the car door, I realized with distress that it was locked. Not only that, but I could plainly see the keys stuck in the ignition.

Quickly, I ran around to the other side of the car and wailed, "Wait, Scott! I've locked the keys in the car again! Now what are we gonna do?"

Scott walked nonchalantly to the driver's side of the rental car and stood in the spot where I'd been standing before my wailing and gnashing of teeth. (He's grown accustomed to this stuff; nothing fazes him anymore.) Then he looked up at me without emotion from across the car's hood and said, "Well, Beck, I guess you could do this." Then he reached through the driver's side window—that had been completely rolled down the *entire time*—pulled the keys out of the ignition, and handed them to me.

"Oh," I said quietly, trying not to smile, "that would be a very good idea."

At a recent football game I walked into one of two unmarked

bathroom doors, hoping against hope that behind Door #1 I'd find a room full of females. Instead I barged in on a row of startled men, scurrying to find their zippers. Embarrassed, I offered a quick apology and exited, grateful that at least now I'd be sure to go in the correct door. Entering Door #2 full of confidence, I could not believe my eyes when I spied the backs of the same startled men lined up in a row. Turns out this was one of those bathrooms with one door for an entrance and one for an exit. And I, the lucky winner, had picked both doors.

"Yes," you say, "but these are weird circumstances you've created yourself, out of your own stupidity. What does this have to do with divine intervention?" I'm getting to that.

Last month I was driving down the road, minding my own business when, a few cars ahead of me, I saw a grocery sack fall out of the back of a pickup truck. (In Texas, you're rarely more than a car's length from a pickup.) I could clearly see that one of the items rolling out of the sack down the highway appeared to be a bottle of shampoo.

Then, like one of those comical car chase scenes in movies, the car in front of me ran smack over that shampoo bottle, whereupon it exploded, depositing its entire contents onto my windshield.

Gabe, my ten-year-old son, was sitting in the front seat beside me. I glanced at him briefly. He said nothing, but his mouth was wide open, and his eyes were darting back and forth from the windshield to me to see what I would do next. I couldn't see a thing through the bluish-green muck, so I turned on my windshield wipers.

At that very moment it started to rain. No kidding. So now I had a foaming bubble bath in full swing, sliding back and forth across my windshield. The more the wipers waved, the more the bubbles foamed. Airborne soap floated and lifted from the windshield in streams as we drove along in the sudden shower. I glanced over at Gabe once again. Still no words were coming from him, but his mouth was a little bit wider, and his eyebrows were so high that they'd now disappeared under his bangs.

As we neared home, I pulled into the driveway, and suddenly the sun burst from behind the clouds—the rain had gone as quickly as it had begun. My windshield was sparkling clean. I rolled down my window, poked my head out, and looking up in the direction of the clouds, said, "Thank you, Lord, You did a great job. I don't think my windshield's ever been this clean before."

Gabe finally found his voice. "Mom," he asked carefully, "do you think these kinds of things happen to other kids' mothers?"

"Honey," I giggled, "I don't know. You see, God has His hand on me."

It makes Scott uncomfortable for me to say things like that, even though he knows I'm just poking fun, because he really believes that I am sometimes too self-absorbed—that I think more highly of myself than I ought to be thinking. That I really believe God would take time off from answering Billy Graham's prayers to personally clean my windshield. (The truth is, I don't think He has to take time away from the big, traumatic prayers to send a little lighthearted sunshine—or rain—to His children. He is *God,* after all.)

Scott is the calm, unruffled type. (I bet you guessed that already. Absentminded, perpetually "ruffled" people always marry their opposites. It's the way God keeps us balanced.) Our senses of humor, especially, are expressed in diverse ways. While I chuckle uncontrollably, telling the latest embarrassing story on myself, my husband often just sits and shakes his head back and forth slowly. The way I can tell he thinks anyone is hilarious— even the funniest comedians—is by closely examining the corners of his mouth. One quarter turn upwards and I know Scott is dying laughing inside. Sometimes, he rolls his eyes toward the ceiling (thinking I don't notice) as I become deeply moved—sometimes to the point of tears—by reading aloud my own writing.

"It's unhealthy, Becky, to be that absorbed in your own little world," he says. "Not to worry," I tell him.

"If creative people weren't self-absorbed," I explain, "we'd *really* drive everyone nuts. This way, we're taking care of our *own* absorption so others don't have to do it *for* us. See how unselfish we really are when you think about it like that?" Scott says he prefers not to think about it at all.

Enough with this talk of self-absorption. Back to more thoughts about me.

The longer I live, the more I realize I'm full of contradictions. Though a deep thinker, I'm also incredibly shallow. I'm quite bright (really, truly I am) but amazingly lacking in common sense. Within the span of five minutes, one friend described me as both spiritually wise and hopelessly naive. I'm curious and studious, but my children will tell you there could not be a more forgetful mother on this earth.

In coming to terms with my own dichotomies, I've drawn special comfort from observing the life of Albert Einstein. Einstein was a classic example of the creative/contradictory personality. Sure, he discovered the Theory of Relativity, but did he ever figure out how to use a comb? Perhaps he just couldn't find it and decided to move on to more interesting things. I, you see, would have empathized and understood this about Albert.

Something else I love about Albert Einstein. He had a brain with a heart. He said amazing things like, "There are only two ways to live your life. One is as though nothing is a miracle. The other is as though everything is a miracle." Albert, bless him, chose the latter view.

I would have loved sitting out on the porch swing trading stories of miracles with Einstein if we had lived in the same neighborhood back then. Of course, who's to say whether either of us would have been able to pay attention to the other long enough to carry on a decent conversation. Einstein probably would have nodded his head politely, pretending to listen to me, when he was really working out the answer to some obscure equation in his mind. And I most likely would have pretended to be listening to his scientific equations while working out in my mind all the styles I could create with that mass of flyaway, cottony hair.

I guess it all boils down to this: Some of us are divinely called to be lights in this dark world. And some of us are called to be really weird people. And I'm finding it strangely restful to simply accept that.

O LORD, you . . . know everything about me . . . when I sit or stand . . . you know my every thought . . . and tell me where to stop and rest.
(Ps. 139:1–3, TLB)

chapter three
NAPPING IN THE BREEZE

My friend Linda, who is a physical therapist and busy mother of three boys, leaned forward over the restaurant table where we were having lunch. "Becky," she said in hushed tones, "the other day I drove up to this dangerous-looking neighborhood to do a home visit, and as I walked toward the front door, I thought to myself, *This is the kind of neighborhood where I could get shot. What if I do get shot?!? What if I get splattered by gunfire right here on the front lawn?*"

Using my best "isn't that special?" Church Lady imitation, I smiled sweetly and replied, "Well, there's a cheery little thought-for-the-day."

"That's the point, Becky," Linda replied, her eyes growing wide. "To me, it *was* a cheerful thought! Because my reflex response to my own question was, 'Hey, if I get shot, at least I'll have a good excuse to lie down and put my feet up for a while.' "

I laughed and said, "Look, Linda, I'm no psychologist, but I'd venture to guess that when a *gurney* starts looking like a cozy spot to curl up on, it's time for a blankey and a pillow and a nice, long nap."

To man's eternal question, "What does a woman really want?" I answer, "A nap. That's all; she just wants a nap." How many of you can identify with this? (If you are pregnant or have a baby or preschoolers, forgive me for even asking. I know, I know. The fact that your eyes are open long enough to read this sentence is a miracle in itself. I'm honored to have you still with me.)

I used to think I didn't have time for such luxuries. A nap? Are you kidding? In the middle of *my* hectic day? Puh-lease. Or I might take one but wake up feeling frazzled and guilty. There was always this fast-forward tape going on in my head, taunting me with a sing-song, "You're getting behind-er. You're getting behind-er." I thought if I just kept doing and doing, staying focused on my "to do" list no matter what—or who—interrupted my day, I could eventually catch up. Then one bright morning, I had this incredible porch swing epiphany and realized the truth. There is no such place as "All Caught Up." It only exists out there in our imaginations with Oz and Santa's Workshop and Never Never Land.

Why didn't our parents tell us this? Perhaps they, too, are still struggling under the illusion that it exists somewhere out there. You may have to grieve a little over the loss of this fairy-tale catch-up land. You'll find it a healthy, cleansing experience though. Because in the long-run, I guarantee you'll be thankful I told you the hard truth right now, before you waste any more time chasing a dream. When you give up on the existence of "All Caught Up," it frees you to do all those wonderful things you were waiting to do until you arrived there. Like, for example, taking a guilt-free nap.

I want you to know what I did this afternoon—an afternoon loaded with deadlines and housework and phone calls and a hundred obligations. Like a movie producer who yells, "Cut!" I walked away from the middle of the action and went outside to my porch swing where I read and prayed and wrote for an hour or so, until I realized that what I really needed was a nap.

The day was gorgeous, and I craved the warmth of sunshine on my skin, so I laid out a quilt on the deck beside my swing, curled up on it, and fell into deep, peaceful sleep. An hour later I woke up refreshed, without a trace of guilt. *Can you believe it?* Believe me, this sort of experience has been a long time in coming.

I will admit, for young mothers and women with out-of-the-home jobs this is not as easy to pull off. But with a bit of finagling you, too, can nap in the sunshine in guilt-free bliss—at least occasionally or in moderation. Young mothers can set up playpens outside in the backyard on beautiful days, lay the baby down to sleep in the shade, and catnap nearby on a lounge chair. Toddlers are tricky though, a real dilemma for their sleep-deprived parents.

Speaking of toddler tricks, did you read about the man who woke up from a nap with a sudden loss of hearing in one ear? True story. He went to the doctor to find out what had happened. Turns out this guy's two-year-old put superglue in Daddy's ear while he was snoozing away on the couch. Aren't preschoolers just *too* precious? The only way I know for parents of toddlers to get a deep, peaceful nap is to hire a wide-awake baby-sitter, preferably with Olympic energy and a high IQ, to stand guard for you. I've heard rumors that in previous generations mothers would give their little tykes a dose of Paregoric to knock 'em out for a couple of hours. But that might get you arrested today. (Of course, there are days—for parents of toddlers—when a nice, quiet jail cell sounds unbelievably enticing.)

Catching a catnap at the workplace is not nearly as difficult, thanks to boring meetings. One fifty-two-year-old businessman discussed his creative career naps. He said, "I love having long and boring business meetings. . . . I sort of get in this posture that makes people think I am listening. I can even nod my head automatically, like one of those toy dogs in the back window of a car, but I really am gone. I just get these ideas, these weird strange ideas, but sometimes they're the best ideas I have. I don't think business could survive without very boring meetings. There would be no time for real creativity without them."

But even at-home workers, with easy access to a couch or a bed, ask themselves, "How can I stop for a nap when I have so much that I should be doing?" Here is the answer: *You get three times as much accomplished in one well-rested hour as you do in three hours of plodding along half-awake. Take an hour to sleep and an hour to work, and you gain a whole extra hour to play with.* Okay, I'll admit, I just made that up. But it's true; I just know in my bones that it is.

For you scientific types, I do have some objective research proving that one nap a day will increase the number of your highly creative periods. It has to do with hypnopomping and hypnogogging. Really. I'm not making this up. It's science.

Like *jubilee, hypnopompic* and *hypnagogic* are playful words. Yet they are real, honest-to-goodness scientific terms used by sleep researchers. (Can't you just imagine a researcher using these words on some poor sleep-deprived patient with the patient sleepily replying, "So what you're telling me, Doc [yawn] is that I'm a [yawn] pompous-gogging hippo?")

Hypnopompic actually refers to that period of time just before we are completely awake, when our mental pictures are a mixture of dream and our own created images. It is considered one of the most productively creative periods. *Hypnagogic,* on the other hand, refers to that time just before we are asleep, when images, again, are a mixture of dreams and thoughts under our control—another highly creative state of mind.

Thomas Edison had an unusual technique for putting the hypnagogic state to work. The authors of *The Creative Spirit* explain his method. "He would doze off in a chair with his arms and hands draped over the arm rests. In each hand he held a ball bearing. Below each hand on the floor were two pie plates. When he drifted into the state between waking and sleeping, his hands would naturally relax and the ball bearings would drop on the plates. Awakened by the noise, Edison would immediately make notes on any ideas that had come to him."

I tried to explain my scientific discovery to my husband the other night, as I arranged a couple of pie tins on the floor beside the couch where I like to doze—but as is often the case, the conversation got a little carried away.

"So you see, Scott," I began, "when I take a nap, I get in a whole extra session of hypnogogging and 'pomping that I would miss otherwise."

"Yeah, well, that's fine," he answered with a mischevious smile, "as long as you save some of that 'pomping and 'gogging for nighttime when you're sleeping with me."

"Don't worry," I teased, kissing his cheek. "I'd rather hypno with you beside me any day."

"Becky?"

"Uh-huh?"

"I just want you to know—well, you make me want to gog."

"Oh, stop it, Scott. You're making me blush." (I think there's something about a woman talking "scientific" that drives men crazy.)

In my researching, I also discovered that the Year of Jubilee is also called the Sabbath Year. It occurred once every seven years, and it means "the year of rest," just like the Sabbath day was God's anointed *day* of rest. If it makes sense to have a day of rest once a week and a year of rest every seven years, would it not follow that there ought to be a short period of rest about every seven hours during the course of a typical day? Most people get sleepy and groggy around 2:00 or 3:00 in the afternoon, right? Well, that's about seven hours after most of us have had our caffeine and consider ourselves to be legally awake. (Before 8:00 A.M. our bodies may be moving, but our minds are still struggling to wake up and smell the coffee.)

In Latin America, they deal with this sleepy midafternoon time by embracing the *siesta*. What a concept! I just had another thought. *Siete* means "seven" in Spanish, right? Well, *siete* and *siesta* sure look a lot alike to me. What are the chances that *siesta* literally translates to mean, "Take a nap every seven hours," or perhaps, "After seven hours of working, you are no good to anybody anyway, so go home to your *casa,* take a *siesta,* and then come back when you're ready to *trabaja*"?

The English have a countrywide, sleepy-time breather they disguise as a tea party. Again it takes place in the late afternoon and they call it *high tea.* Now once again, I'm no translator, but I have a feeling in my bones (and my bones are incredibly perceptive when they're well rested) that the English term *high tea* literally means, "After seven hours of working, you're no longer a jolly whit of good. So pop over to your flat, have a spot of tea, take a short nap, then come round when you're functioning properly again."

One of the most famous of all English writers, William Shakespeare, didn't even use high tea as a cover-up for napping. He gave it public adulation, penning the words, "Oh, beloved nap time, nature's soft nurse."

I wish someone would explain why, if we are such a brilliantly advanced nation, American forefathers let the concept of a nationwide naptime slip through the cracks of the Constitution? At least Ronald Reagan was bright enough to catch on. I think his naps made him a Jubilee kind of president. I, for one, miss having him in the Oval Office. His mere presence was soothing, even when he was snoozing.

In his honor, I'd like to propose a constitutional amendment that would set aside a specific time for patriotic American naptaking. We could call it the Jubilee Hour. I don't know though. When I look at it written out like that, the Jubilee Hour makes me picture "gospel quartet" more than "nationwide nap." Perhaps we ought to call it Hypnopomping-gognapping, which loosely translates to mean, "I'm getting so tired I'm not making sense anymore." Think I'll go back out to my quilt and let my head dry out in the sun 'til I can think clearly again. Maybe I'll even get a little more shut-eye—just until the feeling comes back in my bones.

I will lie down and sleep in peace.
(Ps. 4:8)

RESTING ON THE RUN

There are those times in life when naps are but a hazy memory, when chaos rains down around us so fast that we only have two options: (1) go nuts trying to fix the rapidly accumulating messes ourselves, or (2) give up and let God have the whole wacky ball of wax. Charlie Shedd shares a family story that I often think about when life gets too tangled for me to tango with. It's a story that was first published in 1962, when I was a mere babe, in a book called *Time for All Things*.

Charlie's daughter, Karen, had been working on an elaborate science experiment: an electronic model of the human brain. The project soon became too complicated for her. (I can't imagine why—how hard can it be for an elementary school kid to create a human brain?) Anyway, she sought help from a neighboring electronic wizard named Ben.

At first Karen tried bringing bits of the project over to Ben's house to get his expert input. But the project only got more confusing. One evening, Karen came home, excited about a new plan she and Ben had worked out. "Ben says I should bring the whole business over to his house. Instead of me taking him the parts, he wants the whole deal. Then he'll give me the parts in their right order." What a great concept to apply to our tangled lives. Give the Master the whole deal, then let *Him* show *us* what to deal with, one thing at a time. After all, He knows where we ultimately want to be. Revealing too much at once only clogs our all-too-human brains.

One of the craziest and most chaotic weeks in recent memory occurred this past summer, when I had a series of nonstop chances to put this one-thing-at-a-time approach into practice.

It all began with a phone call from a good friend of mine, Shawn. "Becky!" she yelled into the phone. "Guess what?! I just got a call from the producer of *The Caryl and Marilyn Show*—you know the show with the two real, live best friends in it? They used to be on that sitcom called *The Mommies?*"

"Oh, yes—I've seen ads for it. Looks like it is going to be a fun show."

"Well, they reminded me so much of you and me that I thought I'd write them a letter and tell them they should interview you on their show! And now Stan, one of the producers, wants to talk to you!"

"You're pulling my leg."

"Nope. Here's his number!"

I said a hurried "Good-bye and pray for me" to Shawn, then dialed the number. Before long I found myself chatting with a real, live Hollywood television producer named Stan.

"Yes, Becky!" Stan exclaimed enthusiastically, "I'm looking at your picture right here on the cover of—is it *Home Life* magazine? I also see you've written a book called *Marriage 9-1-1*—right?"

"Well, yes. . . ."

"You aren't a therapist or anything are you?"

"No—"

"Good. Because Caryl and Marilyn aren't wild about professional know-it-all therapists."

"In that case I should be safe. I'm not a professional anything, and I don't know much."

Stan laughed, and we ended up talking for nearly an hour. He'd name a chapter title from the book, and I'd give him a short blurb or story explaining what it was about. I guess I proved I could at least keep a conversation going because he finally said, "OK, I'm convinced. Let's do the show! Can you fly in the day after tomorrow?"

"Sure!" I answered, as I mentally zoomed by the thousand things I'd have to do in two days: make arrangements for the kids, cancel appointments, get my nails done, purchase a nice suit, and lose twenty pounds so I'd look thin in the nice suit I would buy. The deal done, all I had to do was send a fax with my bio and some questions—by the following evening—to Stan's office in Hollywood. No problem.

Until, that is, my temperamental computer decided to have a nervous breakdown the next afternoon, refusing to process one more word, much less tackle a fax. I'd have to hurry to town and use the fax service at the office supply store before they closed for the day. Running out the front door, papers in hand, I ran smack into my teenage son, Zeke.

"Mom!" he yelled, as I tried to brush by him in my rush to get going. "Can you give me a ride down the road so I can mow the neighbor's grass?"

"OK," I hollered back over my shoulder, "but I've got to hurry. I've got to get a fax off to Hollywood within two hours."

"Great. And Mom—can you please, please, please let me back the station wagon out of the driveway? I'm getting really good at it, and I need the practice driving."

"Zeke, this is not a good—"

"Please, Mom?"

"OK, OK. But let's go!"

Zeke slid into the driver's seat, peered around his shoulder to make sure the coast was clear, and expertly backed the car out of the driveway—and then lodged it squarely on top of a railroad tie.

"Oh, Zeeeeeeeeke!" I wailed.

"Ooops," he said. For the next forty minutes he and I slid around on our bellies in the dirt trying to dig, pry, and cajole the car into moving. After we'd been working on the railroad tie for what seemed like all the livelong day, a familiar man pulled up in his giant-sized pickup.

Out of the truck strolled our hero—a long, tall Texan with a Stetson, a friend of the family named Dallas. "Havin' some trouble, Darlin'?" he asked, sizing up our dilemma. Normally, I'm not wild about being called "Darlin'," but at this point I chose to overlook it. This was no time to assert any feminist leanings. I was, after all, at this moment, a classic damsel in distress. If Dallas could help me out of this fix, he could call me "Darlin' " anytime. Looking for all the world like John Wayne, Dallas sauntered to the back of his pickup, pulled out the biggest jack I've ever seen (they really do make things big in Texas), and in no time at all my station wagon's wheels were back on solid ground.

"Thank you so much!" I shouted sincerely. Dallas tipped his hat and turned to leave.

"Yep, Little Darlin'," he said in parting, "now you're *undid.*" Big D had no idea how "undid" I was becoming. After dropping Zeke off at his lawn, I sped into town and faxed the document. That accomplished, I zipped into the mall to pick up last-minute items: hose, jewelry, breath mints, a new computer. Hoping I could slide that last purchase by my husband as quickly as the salesman had talked me into buying it, I telephoned him from the mall to initiate the breaking-in process.

"Scott?"

"Yes?"

"Um, this is Becky."

"Uh-huh?"

"I just wanted to tell you that I'm on my way home. And I'll also bring home a pizza and a new computer. Do you want Dr. Pepper or Coke to go with that?"

"I guess Dr. Pep—you bought *what?!?*"

"Dr. Pepper it is! See you when I get home!"

I felt fairly safe in assuming that Scott would not want to start a fight over a tiny, whimsical purchase the night before I went on my first big television debut. All my errands done, I rushed home thinking about all I still had to accomplish that evening. That old "You're getting behind-er" voice was ringing in my head at full volume. There was laundry to do, and I still hadn't packed my things or washed my hair. I had to get everything done that night in order to leave the house by 5:30 A.M. and make it to the airport in time. Lost in thought as I drove, I hadn't noticed the storm clouds gathering. Rain began falling in thick sheets. When I pulled up in the driveway, the rain was coming down hard and heavy. It was completely dark outside.

Then something else caught my attention as I glanced toward the house. It was completely dark *inside.* The storm had knocked out our electricity (a common occurrence in these boonies). Without electricity, there would be no lights. Without lights I could not see to pack. Without electricity, there would be no washing machine or dryer—so there would be no clean laundry. Without electricity, there would be no blow-dryer or curling iron—so I would look like a rain-soaked ragamuffin even if I did manage to wash my hair in the darkness.

A View from the Porch Swing

I'd come to a place we all face at frantic times like this: Would I now run around the house screaming in panic about the unfairness of this happening before my big day—or would I light a candle, get in my pj's, take Karen Shedd's advice, and give the whole messy enchilada to God?

Cast all your anxiety on him because he cares for you.
(1 Pet. 5:7)

chapter five

WINGING IT
ON A PRAYER

I walked into the dark house and grinned at the sight of Scott and the kids huddled around a lantern, playing cards. The lights in the house were off, but a light in my head went on.

God, I prayed silently, *You obviously orchestrated this opportunity. You used a handwritten letter from a friend to open a door—into motion picture city, no less. So if You turned the electricity off for now, I'm going to take it as a divine signal that I need to slow down and get some sleep. Wake me up when You are ready for me, and I'll try to take the pieces of this whole experience one step at a time. And Lord, would You mind helping Scott overlook that computer in the back seat of my car?*

The electricity popped on around 4:00 A.M. It was easy to tell because every appliance that had been going when the storm hit came roaring back to life. Blinding lights shone in every room, the dishwasher hummed, the microwave "pinged," the radio blared. With all the mechanical activity going on, I was up, bathed, dressed, and packed for the trip in record time.

Scott escorted me to the airport, and I was grateful to note I had time to spare. When I calmly boarded the plane and found my seat, I realized I was going to fly all the way to California seated next to Miss America. My seatmate had long, silky brunette hair, perfect teeth, lashes a mile long, and an hourglass figure draped in a tailored, red suit. She was the sort of gorgeous that people assume only happens on movie screens. She wasn't really Miss America, but she certainly could have been.

Lord, you know I really prefer to sit next to people who are bigger and uglier than me, I started to whine, but then I remembered my promise to allow Him to order the events in my day. Surviving a trip next to a beauty queen was apparently the piece He was handing me to deal with right now.

"Hello," I said, forcing my friendliest smile.

"Hello," the Ravishing One smiled back nervously. I noticed her red nails digging deep into the arms of the airplane seat. We hadn't even taxied away from the gate yet.

"Nervous about flying?" I asked.

"Petrified."

"This time last year I was terrified of flying too," I said, surprised to hear sincere sympathy in my voice, "but I had to go by myself on a business trip—something I'd never done before."

"Talk to me. Keep talking," she said abruptly. "Tell me everything about it. Listening to you talk might keep me from screaming and running down the aisle and out the exit ramp."

"Okaaaay," I answered slowly. *This should be interesting.* I decided I'd better not question her orders and dove right in with an impromptu monologue. "Well, on that trip I was telling you about—I was going to Nashville and ended up sitting next to the most interesting man. An orthopedic surgeon. He even invited me to come watch him operate on a country music star's knee the next day."

"No kidding!" she exclaimed. Obviously, my distraction was working.

"And get this: We found out he and I were second cousins!"

"No!"

"Yes!"

"I mean—No! They're starting down the runway! I don't want to be on this airplane!"

"Everything will be fine," I said gently, as I observed the panic rising in her face. Suddenly she was no longer a gorgeous model— she was a frightened little girl in need of assurance. I gently placed my hand on her arm in a gesture of sisterly comfort, looked her squarely in the eye, and asked, "Do you believe in prayer?"

"Yes! Are you a Christian too?!?" she nearly yelled.

"Yes—and I prayed that God's angels would help fly our plane. I always try to imagine one on each wing tip—you might try that."

Once we reached cruising altitude, the color crept back into my new friend's face, and she relaxed her grip on the armrests.

"So what made you take this flight?" I asked, settling back in my seat. I was curious about what would cause her to brave this experience.

"I'm on my way to a convention to be with my sister," she answered, a twinge of sadness in her voice. "She has a rare skin disorder. It distorts her face—pulls her skin tightly across her muscles like a stretched balloon. It's very painful and even life-threatening. She used to be stunning—and now . . ." She paused for a moment, then continued, "Well, to me she's more beautiful than ever. She's a wonderful mother, and she's been so brave through this whole ordeal. The least I could do was go with her to this medical convention. There will be lots of people there with her condition. Hopefully we'll find some help."

As my new friend talked, I could see the compassion in her eyes, the love that compelled her to face her terror of flying. When I told her I was on my way to do a television interview about marriage, she opened up about aches in her own marriage and her lifelong battle to find self-esteem. I told her it was hard to imagine her ever battling feelings of inferiority.

"I always felt so dumb," she said. "And the truth is, I never had a surplus of common sense."

"Oh boy," I answered, smiling, "have you got a sympathetic ear here. I've made a whole career out of writing about the stupid things I've done."

"My husband says I'm crazy like a fox. He thinks I'm doing all these ditzy things to get attention. He just cannot comprehend I could be such an airhead—unless I was doing it on purpose. I'm at a loss as to how to explain it to him."

So there we were: two airborne airheads. By the time the jet landed we'd officially bonded and parted company promising to pray for each other's special day. I'd been taught a warm and important lesson, one I'd been needing to learn for a long time. I've often joked about it, but in truth I have often avoided getting to know beautiful women because my self-esteem couldn't handle the contrast between their perfection and my obvious imperfections. God was showing me that hurting people come in all packages—and that I'd been holding on to what I'd assumed was a legitimate prejudice: After all, aren't all normal women allowed to be jealous of those among us who look like Barbie?

No, God was saying to my heart that morning, *you are not. Becky, I want you to come to the place where you see past all outward appearances and begin seeing what I see in people—their hearts.*

Once at the airport I looked around and found the limo driver holding up a sign with my name on it. Again, I asked God to help keep my eyes focused on the journey—especially on people and not on the "performance" ahead. Still there were plenty of butterflies winging their way around my stomach.

The limo driver turned out to be an aspiring screenwriter. (I was to learn that 95 percent of the people driving limos and waiting tables in Hollywood are aspiring screenwriters or actors.) He told me a little about his wife and crew of kids, then asked me about my book. I shared the Cliff's Notes version of its contents. Then, when we came to a stoplight, he turned around and said, "I have a question for you: How do you know when it's time to give up on a marriage?"

"Well," I answered, "I suppose there are times when you have to let go—if the other person walks away, you can't force them to stay. But I know one thing: You shouldn't give up on a marriage just because love dies. Nearly every marriage comes to a point, somewhere along the line, where it feels like the love has died. You just have to find a way to resurrect it."

Apparently, this was a radical thought. I left him with a puzzled look on his face and a copy of *Marriage 9-1-1* on the front seat.

"Break a leg, Becky," the driver said kindly, holding the door open for me as I exited the car. "I'll see you again when the show's over."

From there I was led into the Viacom Studio, smack in the middle of Sunset Boulevard. What kept surprising me about "tinsel town" was how old it was, and how very *unglamorous*. Though the weather is perfect, the sky has an ever-present haze that puts a murky damper on Hollywood's glitz. Even the studio—especially from the outside—reminded me of an aging school building. But I was greeted by the friendliest of staff assistants who did their best to put me at ease. The butterflies were settling a bit.

As soon as I'd been all dolled up by the makeup artists (it's amazing the things they can do with a little paint), I got to sneak into the studio early and watch them do a few preshow "takes" of *Caryl and Marilyn.* Caryl was sitting on the kitchen set, reading a book. Her job this morning was to put down the book and scream (I've now forgotten why) while stagehands pulled up on invisible strings connected to portions of her hair. The result: a "hair-raising scream." *These two gals have quite the interesting jobs,* I thought to myself.

I was pleased to see how at ease Caryl and Marilyn really were—both with each other and the crew. The friendship you see on television is real. It would have to be to survive the long hours they've spent together over the years.

Later, in the greenroom, I met the other guests Stan had pulled together for today's show on "9-1-1 Emergencies." It looked to be an interesting lineup. I was there to deal humorously with marriage crises; another couple was on to share how umbilical cord blood was being used to save the lives of their children; one of the stars of the popular TV show *ER* was there to showcase her jazz singing talents—but the true star of the show was "The Cat Who Dialed 9-1-1."

I met Deputy Joe Bamford, the first officer on the cat-scene, and got the real scoop straight from the source. Dark hair, quick smile, dressed in full law enforcement regalia; I liked Deputy Bamford immediately. Sure, he was a regular "Joe," but I could tell he also took his small-town law duties seriously.

"Can you tell me what happened?" I asked him, feeling like a news reporter.

"Well, yes," Deputy Bamford began, his voice turning serious. "I was on patrol when I heard the cat call come in over the radio. The victim was obviously suffering from some sort of trauma."

"How could you tell?" I asked.

"The 'meow, meows' were distressful in nature." I stifled the laugh threatening to bubble up out of my mouth. I could see this was no laughing matter to the officer.

"I see," I managed to answer solemnly.

"Yes, well, we have to take every call seriously—you just never know. Might have been a cat, but it might have been a woman—"

"Or it might have been Cat Woman." I couldn't resist.

He continued, ignoring my comment. "The dispatcher traced the call and directed me to the location of the feline's house. I found the caller in the home, lying on the floor, flea collar lodged in its mouth. It was pulling the cat's jaw down to the proximity of its chest, causing the animal considerable discomfort. I, of course, moved to release the obstruction immediately. We later discovered that the cat had somehow landed on a telephone button that had been preset to dial 9-1-1—thereby alerting us to its predicament."

"Wow," I grinned, "Now that's a *story.*"

"That's not even the half of it," the deputy continued. "My phone hasn't stopped ringing in two weeks. The cat, its owner, and I have been interviewed all over America, on BBC—I even got a call from Bombay, India, the other day."

"Did you ever think you'd become famous like this?" I quizzed.

"No, my life has been pretty uneventful up to this point." For the first time in our conversation, Deputy Bamford dropped the "officer of the law" demeanor and grinned—big—like a kid who'd won a "get-out-of-school" pass to go play at the beach. "But I have to admit, it's really been kind of fun."

At that point, the assistant producer poked her head around the corner and informed the deputy, cat & company that it was time for their interview. During the next hour and a half, I had several delightful visits with guests, watching them leave and then viewing their segments on the video screen in the waiting area. Then came the big moment: My turn was up next.

Just then Stan came around the corner looking as though he'd just heard I'd caught a fatal disease—such was the pain in his eyes. "Becky," he said, "I'm so sorry! But the show ran too long. There's no time for your segment."

You mean I've been bumped by a long-winded cat? I thought, shaking my head in disbelief. *These things only happen to me.*

The butterflies in my stomach that had finally begun flying in formation landed with a sickening thud. *So Lord, what's this day been about? I thought I came all this way to talk about my book on a television show and now*—I swallowed the initial disappointment and graciously thanked Stan for inviting me anyway. He turned sadly and walked away. At that point, Caryl and Marilyn came bustling around the bend all aflutter. I smiled and shook their hands as they both began profusely apologizing at once, talking over each other just the way they do on camera. I felt like I was in the middle of a sitcom.

"Really," I interrupted, suddenly feeling more at peace about the whole thing. "It's *fine.* These things happen. I could have spent the day doing lots less exciting things than I got to do today. I had a great trip out here, and I loved meeting you and the other guests."

At that point, Caryl dropped to her knees, took my hand, and said, "Thank you, thank you, *thank you* for being so nice about this!"

"So some people aren't?" I asked.

The famous friends looked heavenward in disgust. "Oh, listen," said Marilyn, gesturing as she talked, "some people actually throw stuff and yell and cuss and storm out of here if they get bumped from the show."

"You're kidding?" Like synchronized swimmers, Caryl and Marilyn swayed their heads from left to right and back again, a silent, animated answer to my question.

Just then, Stan flew into our circle, his face exuberant, his hands flying. "Becky! Can you come back on Friday?"

"Well, I think so."

"Great. Listen, I want you to meet another producer—Ginger. She'll talk to you about doing Friday's show."

As I walked from the studio to the waiting limo, the driver looked up and smiled. "Becky, I've got something to tell you."

"What?" I asked as he opened the door.

"Well, while you were in the studio, I was reading your book," he leaned on the hood, then winked down at me. "I also made a phone call to my wife to tell her how much I loved her."

So why did I end up wasting a whole day flying out to L.A., only to end up postponed and having to do the complicated routine all over again? This was not the simple, laid-back week I'd envisioned before Shawn's phone call. I can think of several reasons.

First of all, there was a frightened woman on a plane who needed a friend. I happened to be free that day, so perhaps God chose to work through me to comfort one of His kids. (And He taught me that beautiful people can have beautiful, frightened hearts.) There was a limo driver who needed to be encouraged that marriage is tough, but it's worth the work to keep it. Then there was the hurried woman who needed to see how faithful God is to bless our days and to use us as His vessels when we let Him lead us one step at a time. He's showing me I can rest on the run. And that people are more important than our destination, for human connections are a large part of the jubilees we'll enjoy on life's journey. Then, too, I've a feeling God knew I'd get a royal kick out of meeting the cat who dialed 9-1-1.

(Not to mention that it gave this anonymous, impulsive woman an opportunity to be three thousand miles away from her husband when he discovered the price tag on that new computer in the backseat of the car.)

If I go up to the heavens, you are there. . . .
if I settle on the far side of the sea,
even there your hand will guide me.
(Ps. 139:8–10)

chapter six

COCOONING IN A CABIN

I am, at this moment, living every mother's fantasy. I'm all alone (going on the third day) in a rustic cabin, in the fall of the year. For three days, I've experimented with what life might be like if I were a single woman—and a hermit. Since I married at the tender age of seventeen and went straight from being someone's daughter to someone's wife, the ways of living alone are as foreign to me as the habits of some ancient tribe in a far-off land. I'd been wondering, especially after a succession of intense, crowded days (like the two I'd just spent in Hollywood), *What would it feel like to live in solitary isolation for awhile?*

Now I know.

It's a little quiet, even a bit lonely, but on the whole—for a short time, at least—it's rather heavenly.

I find it fascinating to be preparing meals for me and me only. I've also pondered, *What would I eat for meals if I were single? What would I buy at the grocery store with only my tastes in mind, left alone to eat whenever and whatever my heart (or tummy) desired?*

So far, I've gone through half a bag of apples, half a pint of caramel dipping sauce (fat free), a bag of chocolate cookies (fat-free), half a can of turkey chili, half a can of baked beans, half a can of bean dip and assorted (fat-free) chips, and two small potatoes. Oh, I did have a salad and some carrots (fat-free) once—thrown in for good measure. My dinnerware has consisted of one sturdy Styrofoam plate, a small, empty butter tub, and a coffee mug. (These, too, may I point out, are fat-free.) The sole utensils in this cabin are a huge serving spoon, a fork, and a steak knife. I have eaten oodles of onions on everything with nary a thought of offending anyone with bad breath. Being a recluse has its perks.

Another thing: There is no reason to put on makeup or even shave my legs. Whom am I going to impress? Whom will I rub up against? I only comb my hair to get it out of my eyes, and I secure it back with whatever is handy—I've discovered a large Chip Clip or a couple of wooden clothespins work great.

I've undergone a rare transformation in these few short days. I'm becoming more than Becky of the Boonies; I'm turning into Wild Nature Woman. I've left the society of Women Who Run with Poodles and joined the pack of Women Who Run with Wolves. All day long yesterday I wore a shirt with a big ketchup stain right in the middle of my stomach. Slept in it last night. Who cares about stains when it's just you and the foliage?

Yesterday the most exciting thing that happened to me was that a huge praying mantis and her mate crawled atop my computer. I put them in a glass container, with the lid slightly ajar, for scientific observation. I heard somewhere that once the female is finished mating with the male she bites his head off. I guess I'll never know. When I woke up this morning, both of them were gone. Maybe they ate each other.

Actually, the subject of male/female difficulties brings me to how I landed in these woods—like some displaced Goldilocks—in the first place. I'm telling everyone that I'm away to write and reflect and catch up on work. (Though, so far, there's been more "ketchup on my work" than "catch up on my work.") If the truth be known, I'm actually in exile. Two days before I landed in the wilderness, I had a semi-nervous breakdown. It worried me because I didn't think it had a thing to do with hormones. Didn't feel like hormones. Just felt as though the world was falling apart, deadlines were looming over me like monsters, and my head was about to explode.

Scott discovered me curled up in the fetal position, crying and sobbing like a baby, saying over and over again, "I just can't do it all!" Another peculiar symptom: Suddenly, I was seized with an overwhelming desire to have my house clean—*spotlessly* clean. *Immediately!* (Me, whose first book described me as the happy, oblivious owner of the "dirtiest floor in America.") Suddenly, one little sock on the floor grated on every nerve in my body. The dust on the coffee table looked as thick and deep as the Sahara desert. It was all so hopeless, hopeless, *hopeless!!!* But I did not think it was PMS.

Scott found me in this pitiful condition and held me with compassion as if I were a child in his arms. Then he immediately set to plotting how he might creatively put me in solitary confinement for a few days. To his everlasting credit (young husbands take note) he did not mention the words *hormones* or *PMS*. Wisely, he said, "Honey, what's wrong with you is that you are worn out. You need time away to regroup, catch up on sleep and your writing.

There's a cabin I know of that you can use for a few days. I'll take care of the kids, and you go and relax. . . ."

"But, Scott," I blubbered, wiping my tears, "I can't possibly leave you and the children. . . ."

"Oh, but I insist, Sweetheart. Really. You need this."

"You are the most giving man I've ever met. I love you so much."

"There, there," he patted my back soothingly. "Can I help you pack your suitcase right now? Warm up the engine of the car?"

That's when I started to get a little suspicious. Scott had the wild look of a male praying mantis desperately trying to save his own head. Obviously this "Momma's Getaway" held significance for the kids too. Maybe they knew instinctively that their mother was on the verge of Wild Womandom, a sight they preferred not to behold at close distance. At this point, who was I to quibble over motives? I was ready to do anything to help relieve the pressure building inside. When I agreed to the isolation, my family gave me a standing ovation.

That very afternoon, I found myself cruising through the countryside amid the brilliant fall trees painted with yellow, orange, burgundy, and chocolate brown leaves. When I arrived at the cedar cabin, I unpacked a few things. Then with some surprise I realized—well, what do you know?—I'd miscalculated my cycle. It *had* been a touch of hormones after all! Then it dawned on me, if this had been Old Testament times, under Levitical law I'd have been routinely exiled like this—"set apart seven days" for "customary impurity."

I used to think, *How awful to be "put away" like you were something disgraceful just because it was your God-ordained female time of the month!* Now, I'm beginning to see the brilliance of such a plan. Oh, I might have protested the injustice of it all on some level if I'd lived back then, but eventually I believe it would have dawned on me that this shunning deal was not a bad arrangement for all concerned. True, the men probably felt slightly superior. But as long as the woman had a week off to go somewhere to sit and relax without having to skin goats or shear sheep or make stew, who cared? Could this have been God's gift to women—a seven-day monthly jubilee?

I keep envisioning that famous children's story where Br'er Rabbit (who'd grown up in the stickers and thickets) pleads with Br'er Bear, "Please, oh, please—just don't throw me in the brier patch!" Only I picture an Israelite woman hiding her smile as she says, "Please, oh, please—you're not telling me I'm unclean are you? What? You want me to just sit? Sit and relax, you say? I can't even lift a tiny finger to cook or clean or scrub pots or milk goats? How *terrible*."

Research indicates that the monthly cycles of women living together in a group (like college dorms or tribes) tend to synchronize until everyone is on the same schedule. Are you thinking what I'm thinking this might have meant for the women of Israel? *Yes!* Most of the women would be ushered off, quite possibly, *together.*

Think about it: Jewish women could do Girl's Night Out, Slumber Party, Women's Retreat, Gobble and Gab—all without a trace of guilt. After all, they were being put away for their "uncleanness." What could they do but stoically make the best of their dire predicament? (Of course, the Israelite men and kids were probably living it up too—belching loudly, leaving manna crumbs and quail bones all over the tent floor.) Whatever the case, after having some time to myself to gather my thoughts, I've come to believe this "setting apart" business may be an old tradition that needs revisiting, whether it takes the form of a women's retreat or a day alone.

In the book *Wouldn't Take Nothing for My Journey Now,* poet and author Maya Angelou discusses the refreshment that comes from taking some downtime for ourselves. She writes, "Every person needs to take one day away. . . . Family, employers, and friends can exist one day without any one of us." Obviously, this was true for my family. They practically threw a parade to celebrate my departure.

Angelou continues, "Each person deserves a day away in which no problems are confronted, no solutions searched for. Each of us needs to withdraw from the cares which will not withdraw from us. We need hours of aimless wandering or spates of time sitting on park benches, observing the mysterious world of ants." (I wonder if mating praying mantises count?)

"If we step away for a time," Maya Angelou contends, "we are not, as many may think and some will accuse, being irresponsible, but rather we are preparing ourselves to more ably perform our duties and discharge our obligations."

Precisely! Does not a battery need to recharge? Does not land need time to lie fallow so that it might better nourish its crops? Do not caterpillars need their cocooning time to morph into butterflies? And doesn't a woman need an occasional jubilee-getaway to refresh her body and soul? I also believe every busy mother occasionally needs some time away in order to experience being hungry for the company of family again. Empty arms, here and again, help us appreciate how sweet two arms can feel when they are once again full of children (or husband).

Well, my time here at the Wild Woman Cabin is coming fast to a close. I must shower (and shave), take the Chip Clip out of my hair so I can wash, roll, and brush it clean. It's time to throw out the onion, brush my teeth, and chew a mint; to forage for a shirt without a tomato-based stain. Time to pack up the car with my books and computer, to say goodbye to the friendly forest and woodland creatures. Though I've thoroughly enjoyed my exile, I am ready for my return home. My arms are beginning to feel strangely empty. I'm also craving communication with something that's not mineral, vegetable, furred, or antennaed.

COCOONING IN A CABIN

"A day away acts as a spring tonic," concludes Maya Angelou. "It can dispel rancor, transform indecision, and renew the spirit."

On this I must agree. I take my leave from this abode with my spirit renewed, indecision transformed, and my raging rancor dispelled throughout the woods instead of all over my family. Goodbye, Wild Nature Woman. I think I'm ready to prance with the poodles again.

Very early in the morning, while it was still dark, Jesus got up,
left the house and went off to a solitary place.
(Mark 1:35)

chapter seven
BLOWING UP THE TV

Funny thing. Though I actually got to *appear* on television, I had to walk over to my neighbor's house to watch the segment when it aired—because we don't have a TV.

Well, that's not altogether accurate. We have a television, but it doesn't work, except to play rented videos. (We still have a VCR.) Remember that John Denver song I loved as a teenager? The one about blowing up the TV and moving to the country and building a home and living off fruit trees? Last year I would have said, "Look. We moved to the country, and we're building a home. We had a lot of children, and I've given them their fair share of peaches. But if you think for one minute that I'm going to blow up the TV, well you're off your Rockies. Erica on *All My Children* is about to reunite with husband #27, and I have to see what happens next." So God made it easy and blew up the TV for us.

Our house was literally struck by lightning—not once, not twice, but three times in one year. Blew out two modems in my computer and knocked out the television three times. After the first two incidences, we had the damaged equipment repaired, but after the third strike, we hesitated. Could this be a sign? I thought about some of our friends who, several years ago, went through quite the "thunder"-ous ordeal.

It happened to my friend Mary and her back-then-husband, Gary. (They've divorced and each remarried now. But that's another story in another book.) Anyway, they went through a particularly trying time within a one-month span. First, Gary, a loan officer, lost his job during the height of the Texas banking industry's cutbacks. Then Mary was hit with a crippling round of mononucleosis. Their beloved Norwegian elkhound, Thor, had to be put to sleep. Finally came the crowning touch—their house was struck by lightning. It blew the phone completely off the wall, scorched a line in their living room carpet, and hit the metal pole of their carport. Leaning against that pole was their last remaining dog, who ended up paralyzed in his hindquarters for several disconcerting days. His name—and I know this is hard to believe— was "Sparky." (Sparky had a full recovery. Until, that is, he was run over by that car. . . .)

Mary laughs about the evening she and Gary sat around adding up all their woes and trying to make sense of the recent events. At one point Mary asked, "Gary, do you think we might be doing something wrong here?" To which Gary deadpanned, "Gee, I don't know. Would you like to ask for a *sign from God?*"

And they had only been struck by lightning once! We'd been hit three times. Sign from God or not, we stalled around and didn't take the television in for repairs on its third strike. The first month, our family went through some pretty strange withdrawal ceremonies. We'd sit in our usual TV watching places around the living room, staring at the black screen as though, if we all concentrated at once on the broken set, it might divinely bounce back to life just as quickly as it had been struck down. We must have looked like a zombie support group. The teenage boys were especially pitiful, fingering the remote control gently, recalling the power they once wielded in the palms of their hands.

I wandered around for two weeks in a state of suspended curiosity. "What happened with Erica and her ex-husband?" Finally, in desperation, I called a friend and asked what had transpired on the show. Nothing significant had occurred in *All My Children* land since the television met its demise that black and stormy night. Erica had hosted a luncheon, bought a new dress at the boutique, and made a couple of dramatic entrances. It was then that I realized that you basically have to watch a soap opera for a good six months before the main characters actually *do* anything. They spend four out of five of their weekdays dillydallying around with insignificant characters—repeating what they just told yesterday's minor characters. What a waste of good time.

Then I realized all the fun things I could do during the designated soap opera hour. It would free up time for one of my favorite activities—going to lunch with friends (without subtly trying to schedule it around my "show"). I could catch up on correspondence or cleaning, go shopping, take a nap, go out to my porch swing and visit with a friend, or read to my heart's content.

Eventually, the whole family started moving again in the evenings, like wooden Pinocchios coming to life. Without the TV's ever-present canned laughter and applause punctuating the background, my head didn't pound anymore. Without the daily bombardment of bad news, all of us grew generally more optimistic about our world. Even our kids noticed it.

As I was driving a car full of teens to church one night, several of the girls began to discuss their fears of the future, of what's "out there." I brightened when Zeke piped up from the backseat and said, "You know what? Since we haven't had a television, the world sure seems like a friendlier place."

Zeke's observation started my brain cells firing (no easy task). I began to wonder about the wisdom of exposing the human psyche to all of the evils going on in the entire world. The news, especially, distorts reality.

What is reality? Reality is that 70 percent of what happens each day could be seen, through grateful eyes, as a beautiful miracle. Twenty percent, I'll grant you, is just blah and boring: brushing your teeth, trimming toenails, wiping down the kitchen counter. Ten percent is disgusting and sad and horrid and evil, and to the best of our abilities we should try to offer what relief and comfort we can to those who are hurting.

But why does the news focus on the revolting 10 percent, making us think that this is the "reality" of the world around us? It's not a true picture. It's a tiny segment of a greater, more positive world. I cannot believe God designed us to take in this much bad news on a regular basis. In this instance, "no news is good news" may prove to be profoundly true. It's no wonder teens often feel afraid and hopeless—even great Christian kids, who have *everything* to look forward to.

I know I'm ascending to dangerous soapbox territory, but I firmly believe each older generation *owes* its children a bright vision of their future. The "new millennials" won't try to improve the world if we make them feel like it's a hopeless cause. I wish I could give every teenager in the country a Bible and a pair of sunglasses with a note attached to it that says,

> You're about to discover in these pages that your future's so bright, you're gonna have to wear shades. So turn

that boob tube off, let the Son shine in, and get out there and glow! After all, "You are the light of the world" (Matt. 5:14).

With Love, from an Old Lady Who's Cheering You On

Welcome to the Freeman Family living room—nine months post-television. You'll still often find us sitting around in our old TV watching spots—now talking and joking with each other. Or you might catch us each doing our own new thing. Zachary took up the guitar (and a part-time job). Zeke discovered the computer and found time to be in a one-act play and run track this spring. Gabe, from months of shooting hoops instead of chilling out in front of the tube, turned into the best basketball player on his team. Rachel's brushing up on her communication skills, spending her free evenings chatting on the phone to her friends. (Ah, well . . .). Scott began work again on remodeling the house, his energy renewed. And me? Well, I haven't taken up cleaning and gourmet cooking. Yet. (There's always hope.) But I did find more time to enjoy the kids and visit with my husband—and to write this book about the complicated ways we're trying to simplify our lives.

I do think there are easier ways to cut back on addictive television watching habits than having lightning strike your house. But our family was one of those who needed more than a gentle nudge. I'm glad God zapped the TV for us, even if it took three times before we got (or should I say *lost?*) the picture.

After all, the world looks much brighter since the screen went dark.

Your lightning lit up the world.
(Ps. 77:18)

chapter eight
SINGING FOR YOUR SOUL

Coffee with rich cream. Turn-of-the-century decor. Linen table-cloth, crystal, silver. Morning sunshine pours through the dining room's Victorian stained-glass window and halos the snowcapped mountains in the distance. And now, my husband of twenty years kisses me good-bye. There is a childlike gleam in his eye, for he is off on an adventure—a day of snow skiing alone without having to worry about me or the children or, for that matter, another living soul.

I meet his eyes with a knowing wink for I, too, am anticipating several hours of delicious freedom. On the lace tablecloth in front of me lies a Belgian waffle, dripping with butter and orange marmalade, and the local paper, a pen, and a journal I'm recording my thoughts in this morning. To my left a handsome waiter (part-time ski buff) stands eager to keep my coffee warm and my breakfasting pleasant. I will spend the afternoon visiting and shopping among the interesting, laid-back people of Durango (or "Durangotangs," as they call themselves). It is the perfect, romantic getaway experience: Each of us doing what we love for the day, then coming back together in the evening for dinner, conversation, and, well, other things. Now I ask you, does life get any better than this?

Yes, it does. Because now the strains of *Pachelbel's Canon in D* are drifting and swelling from somewhere above and behind my head. Let Scott have his slopes with fresh powder; I'm having my own personal "Rocky Mountain High" inside the Strator Hotel Restaurant, enveloped by this beautiful piece of music. Involuntarily, tears spring and fall as quickly as I wipe them from my cheek.

Pachelbel's Canon (or as my kid's say, "Taco Bell's Cannon") is a surefire tear trigger for me, transporting me to a memory so dear that I relive it again in my mind as if it were happening now. I can almost feel myself standing in the small chapel near the back of a beautiful sanctuary, helping my little sister, Rachel, arrange her wedding train. Our mom, the other bridesmaids, and I are laughing and chatting when, suddenly, the bride takes hold of her train (and the proverbial *reins*). Putting her finger to her mouth she whispers, "Shhhh!" Then quietly, her dark curls glistening against ivory satin, black eyes shining, my sister says, "Listen! It's my wedding music. I want to absorb everything about this moment right now." We freeze, like a posed arrangement of wedding dolls, listening as the music of *Pachelbel's Canon* crafts this special moment into our collective memories.

"More coffee?" The waiter's question startles me back into the present.

"Yes, please, with cream and sugar." Sipping my coffee slowly, I pause to sigh and realize this is not the first time I've felt transported by this particular piece of music.

A few years after that day, when I watched my sister become Mrs. Rachel Scott St. John-Gilbert III (I know, I also think it's a bit much), I purchased a tape of classical music, popped it into my car stereo, and set out on my daily drive to pick up my children from school. *Pachelbel's Canon* began to play, and in my mind I was no longer in my station wagon. I imagined myself back in that stained-glass church, watching my beautiful sister float out of the dressing room to the strains of this lovely music and down the aisle toward her groom. I could barely see the road, the sentimental tears were flowing so fast and so free. When the song ended I looked up with a start and found that I was in an unfamiliar town—I'd missed the exit to my children's school by over ten miles. The children looked bewildered when, thirty minutes late to pick them up, I explained, "I'm sorry. You see, I was at your Aunt Rachel's wedding five years ago."

Shortly after the "missed exit" experience I visited my sister at her home in Virginia. One afternoon we went shopping at a mall and wandered together into a music store. Suddenly, *Pachelbel's Canon* began playing over the sound system.

"Rachel," I whispered loudly, "listen!"

"Oh, yes," she answered, a smile of remembrance spreading, her dimples deepening. "It's my wedding song."

"I know, I know! Oh, Rachel, did I write you about the time when I started listening to this piece in my station wagon, and I was supposed to pick up the kids but got so carried away with the music that the next thing I knew I'd missed . . ."

"Becky, you're starting to cry!"

"Oh, I know [sniff] you'll all just have to ignore me. I do this. Wait a minute. I'm OK [pause] No, never mind. I'm losing it again. . . ."

"Becky, it's OK. Settle down. Remember, you were going to tell me what happened in your station wagon?"

"Oh, yes. Well, I was listening to this Canon. Is this not the most beautiful music you've ever heard? Oh, dear. I don't think I can finish the story; I'm getting choked up again."

At this point a nearby group of milling people were beginning to stop and stare. Through my watery eyes and sniffs I looked at Rachel, then at the small crowd around us, laughed, and using my best Brooklyn accent said, "I'll be all right. Just tawlk amongst yuhselves for a moment while I pull myself togethuh."

I never did manage to get the story out. Rachel gave up waiting for my sentimental tears to ebb and decided it would be more prudent to simply move me on down the mall towards Dillard's— significantly less emotional territory than a music store. I noticed she was also careful to steer me away from Things Remembered and Hallmark.

What can I say? I'm a sap when it comes to music. Especially romantic or patriotic music. Or bluegrass. Or soft jazz. Or those cute, little kiddy songs on the *Wee Sing* or *Veggie Tales* tapes. It's as if the notes enter my ears, go straight to my tear ducts, and yell, "Now! Turn on the faucets!"

Recently, Scott and I attended a banquet for about three hundred bank CEOs and their wives in Tupelo, Mississippi. I was invited there, believe it or not, to speak. (Yes, life is full of quirks: Author of *Worms in My Tea* meets The Banking Institution.) After my talk Scott joined us for the banquet, where a music group was providing the evening's entertainment. At its close, the lights went down low, and one of the performers, a baritone, gently sang a moving rendition of "I'll Be Seeing You." Certain strains of the song brought sweet memories of my grandmother, Nonnie, into my mind, and, predictably, the waterworks began to flow.

Honestly, I hate my "musical crying" personality disorder; it's so inconvenient. I'd love to simply appreciate and absorb a touching piece of music—perhaps wipe away a delicate tear and be done with it. But I can't. For some reason, I flood. Since I was seated at the head table, there was no place to escape for a private tear-letting. After I'd soaked my napkin, Scott lent me his. Then the bank president's wife handed me hers. By the time I was dotting at my eyes with the corner of the tablecloth, the song mercifully came to an end.

Then the lights went up, and there I sat, blinking at a sea of finance executives, looking like an overwrought raccoon. At this point, I'm sure Scott felt like saying, "Hey, I'll be seeing *you,* Babe," but he stood bravely by my side. At least until he had wiped the mascara from my cheeks, chin, and neck. Then he pointed me toward the lobby and disappeared quickly from view.

Once in the lobby, I ran into the sentimental crooner and began to tell him how deeply I'd been affected by his song. He was flattered, of course, at least until there was a short pause in our conversation and we overheard Scott, directly behind us, chatting with a lovely, sequined soprano.

"Yeah, well," Scott was saying, as he chuckled amiably with the lady, "tell your buddy over there not to get a big head over any of my wife's compliments. I once took her and the kids to Show Biz and found her sobbing all over her pizza because she'd just heard 'America the Beautiful'—sung by a robotic gorilla."

Embarrassed, I whirled around and blurted, "Scott, that gorilla had really sincere-looking eyes!" So much for the baritone's brief moment of glory.

Music began wrapping its arms around me at an early age. I think it started when I was in the second grade and my parents took me to see *The Sound of Music.* My eyes were wide, absorbing the opening scene—the incredible, lush, green Alps covering the entire length of the screen, and then Maria, her arms open wide to the heavens, twirling in childlike joy, singing at the top of her lungs. It dawned on me for the very first time that music comes from heaven and we bounce it back.

A few Sundays ago, a phrase from the hymn "And Can It Be" struck me anew: "My chains fell off; my heart was free—For, my God, *it found out me!*" The hymn writer painted a word picture so intense that as the music pounded majestically from the organ and piano and congregation, the response of my heart to such an incredible gift increased—and of course, the tears poured. *"Amazing love! How can it be That Thou, my God, shouldst die for me?"*

A woman behind me—a fellow music lover—understood my predicament, tapped me on the shoulder, split her Kleenex with me, and mumbled, "Good writing, isn't it?" Even recalling the hymn's words and humming the melody now causes tears to fall down my cheeks again. Here in my office, in privacy, I don't mind the fact that my emotions hover so near the surface. It lets me know that I am alive, that my child-heart is not calloused to His love. I never want to stop *feeling*. And I suppose I'd rather suffer the occasional embarrassment of being thought overemotional than have numb ears. After all, Scriptures are chock full of emotion.

I believe if I could examine all of the Bibles the world over and find the pages that are most rubbed and worn, the most tear-stained, and the most loved, I feel sure those pages would be from the Book of Psalms. Why? Perhaps because this book has been our emotional echo—we find in its poetry something that cannot be explained in logic. The Epistles satisfy our need for spiritual order and logic, but the Psalms have a way of bypassing our heads and embracing our hearts. I find it fascinating that throughout the centuries, men and women have been most drawn to this *musical* book—this set of lyrical works originally intended to be sung and played rather than spoken, lyrics that have comforted us through untold sufferings as well as put words to our joy overwhelming. When I read a psalm, I like to imagine how it might have sounded coming from David's throat on a starry night, accompanied by the peaceful strumming of his harp and the soft bleating of sheep.

One of the sweetest passages I've ever read concerning an encounter with music came from Corrie ten Boom's book, *Tramp for the Lord.* She described the day she was released from her torturous years in a Nazi concentration camp. God used music as a way to bring out Corrie's pent-up emotions—to allow her to fully express her relief and gratitude.

> Far in the distance I heard the sound of a choir singing and then, oh, joy, the chimes of a carillon. I closed my eyes and tears wet my pillow. Only to those who have been in prison does freedom have such great meaning.
>
> Later that afternoon one of the nurses took me up to her room where for the first time in many months I heard the sound of a radio. Gunther Ramin was playing a Bach trio. The organ tones flowed about and enveloped me. I sat on the floor and sobbed, unashamedly. It was too much joy. I had rarely cried during all those months of suffering. Now I could not control myself. My life had been given back as a gift. Harmony, beauty, colors and music.

The season of Jubilee was literally trumpeted into being with the blast of a musical instrument in order "to proclaim liberty throughout the land." It must have been a time of tremendous excitement, particularly for those who'd been enslaved and were now about to taste freedom again. Their thoughts must have paralleled Corrie ten Boom's, for "only to those who have been in prison does freedom have such great meaning." How fitting that this period of freedom, rest, and healing was accompanied by music. How fitting that down through the ages we celebrate birth and birthdays, marriage and death, Easter and Christmas and New Year's with music and song. It is no wonder that God placed musicians in His temples.

Out of curiosity one day, I decided to search out the first and last songs recorded in the Bible. What I discovered was like stumbling upon hidden treasure. The first song in the Bible is found in Exodus, chapter 15; the last song is in Revelation, also chapter 15. The first song is the Song of Moses leading the children of Israel to freedom out of Egypt's slavery. The last? It is sung by saints who've triumphed over Satan's slavery, and they are singing—get this—the Song of Moses *and* the Song of the Lamb. Isn't that incredible? The first and last songs in Scripture, both songs of freedom into light from a dark night of slavery, are woven together in a majestic musical moment to end all moments!

Not only is music filled with spiritual and emotional meaning, it is good for our physical bodies. Consider the following tidbits of scientific news:

- When music was provided in the critical care units of one hospital, they found that "half an hour of music produced the same effect as 10 milligrams of Valium. Also patients who had not been able to sleep for as long as three to four days fell into a deep sleep listening to music." (Take two arias and call me in the morning?)

- Most things with which we humans preoccupy ourselves only involve and activate one side of the brain. (At least I know I've personally been accused, many times, of doing things with half a brain.) But Deforia Lane, author of *Music as Medi-*

cine, says that music is so powerful because "it transcends both sides, so I think not only does it stimulate the language center and the intellect but the emotions and the creative side of our brains as well."

- Elderly patients respond amazingly well to music therapy; they could recall every word to "Amazing Grace" even when they couldn't remember their own birthdays or hometowns.

  (Boy, do I believe this. In the year just before my ailing and fragile grandfather died, he exhausted a room filled with his children, grandchildren, and great-grandchildren by giving us all a thorough trouncing in the musical game "Name That Tune." Granddaddy had played drums in a band from the forties and had a reputation for being quite suave on the dance floor. It was an absolute delight to watch our aging, sickly patriarch perk up as he found new energy to whistle, sing, and even snap out tunes from his heyday.)

- In one study, when soothing music was piped into a post-operative recovery room, the amount of sedative required by the patients was cut in half. One patient was quoted as saying, "I heard *Pachelbel's Canon* when I awoke, and it was such a nice, underlying thing." Not your typical recovery room comment. I think the more standard comment is something like "Who's spinning the room?"

- When Brahms's Lullaby was prescribed for premature infants as part of an experiment, the results were incredible. The infants gained weight faster and went home a week sooner than the babies who didn't hear the music. A savings of $4,800 per infant!

So much for the statistics. Let's get personal again. Do you have a favorite spot on a tape, record, or CD that you've nearly worn out over the years? (By the way, this question makes a great conversation starter.) Like everyone else, I have a couple of my own. One is a song sung by a boy's choir on Michael W. Smith's Christmas album. It is called "All is Well" and is perhaps the most beautiful chorale I have ever heard. Many times, I've literally dropped to my knees in worship as this song swells to fill the room. Kathy Troccoli's album *Sounds of Heaven* is another of my all-time favorite albums filled with beautiful songs. "Go Light Your World" inspires me everytime I hear it, but my favorite is a slow, gentle song of praise called "Hallelujah." (I tend to go for soft and gentle in my old age.) A new just-for-fun favorite is Art Garfunkel's latest CD, *Songs from a Parent to a Child*, dedicated to children.

So what's the porch swing point of this musical discussion? In your darkest nights, in your brightest joys, in your humdrum days, seek out and find your daily dose of music. Oliver Wendell Holmes said, "Take a music bath once or twice a week for a few seasons, and you will find that it is to the soul what the water-bath is to the body."

So turn on some soft, classical music at dinner tonight—even if dinner is McDonald's drive-thru and you have to use your car stereo. Drag the guitar or banjo out to the porch swing this weekend and watch the neighbors come a-calling. Find a foot-stomping bluegrass, rock 'n' roll, or country song to help turn your vacuuming or dishwashing into a Housework Jubilee. Or light a candle in the bedroom, turn on some sexy jazz, and watch your spouse melt into a lover.

And don't forget to bounce some music, as a form of praise,

back to heaven. You may be amazed with the results. "Sometimes a light surprises the Christian when he sings," one hymnwriter wrote. "It is the Lord who rises with healing in His wings."

David would take a harp and play it. . . . Then Saul would become refreshed and well.
(1 Sam. 16:23, NKJV)

BOTCHING IT BIG TIME

chapter nine

If ever there was a time when I made a mess of everything I touched, this was the Botching It Badly Week to top all weeks.

It began Monday night when I agreed to do something totally out of my league, light-years removed from my natural talents. If I'm honest with myself, that may be partly why I agreed to do it; it's hard for me to dodge a challenge. Besides, I believe God likes using the most unlikely people to accomplish His purposes. It keeps everybody on their toes and slightly amazed.

The closer I get to age forty the more I find myself following the advice of a popular speaker, Susie Humphrey: Just volunteer! You can learn it later. Only now I've added my own motto to hang up alongside Susie's: Volunteer! If you blow it badly, the next time you could be told that the best thing you can do to "help the cause" is to stay home and take care of yourself. Either way, you win.

Anyway, on the particular Monday under discussion, a parachurch organization called Young Life was hosting a fund-raising banquet. (Aside: Does the word *parachurch* make anybody else picture a steepled building dangling from a parachute? My mind works like this all the time, but I've discovered it can frighten people, so I mostly keep it to myself.) Anyway, the Sunday before the banquet a pair of leaders cornered me at church and said, "Hey, Becky, we've got a favor to ask. We need someone to give the financial pitch—the closure—for our fund-raising banquet. It's the most important part of the evening, really. But it should be very simple, just a three-to-five-minute deal. We think you'd be perfect."

I raised one eyebrow suspiciously. "Financial pitch? You do know I think balancing my checkbook means keeping it level so it won't fall out of my purse. I'm not exactly what you'd call a financial wizard. I'm probably not even what you could call a financial munchkin."

"That's OK. Really, this won't be a big deal, and you'll be helping a tremendous ministry reach out to high school kids."

"Ooooh. I get it. You couldn't get anyone else to do this, so you're asking me, right?"

"Right."

"OK, that makes me feel much better. Your expectations can't be all that high then. What do I do?"

"Why don't we meet tomorrow for breakfast, and we'll brief you?"

"Right," I answered. Then wanting to add a touch of business savvy, I added, "And I'll try to bring some briefs for you too."

They gave each other a puzzled look, and I walked away

wondering if these folks had any idea what they were taking on. But if they were brave enough to ask, I was willing to give being an overnight financier my best shot.

The Official Briefing took place at the International House of Pancakes because Jim, the main leader, had some great coupons. Jim and his wife, Terry, got right down to business, doing an admirable job of outlining the resources and challenges of the ministry on the back of a menu, but bless their hearts, they had no way of knowing how morning-impaired I am. The main thought on my mind, as I struggled to focus on the scribbled figures, was, *Where's that cheery, blue-aproned waitress with the big pot of coffee anyway? If somebody will give me caffeine immediately, I might not conk out on this little plate of butter pats.*

To further add to my distraction, one of the Young Life assistant leaders, Kelly, had come along for the ride (and for the buy-one-get-one-free breakfast coupon). This is a good place to mention that a qualification for working with a high school ministry is that one must be skilled at performing a great variety of stupid kid tricks. This morning, Kelly was in rare form.

The coffee had finally arrived, and I was slowly coming to life. Jim and Terry and I were busily chatting while Kelly, who was sitting next to me, began nonchalantly peeling the pulp out of a lemon slice. Then—unseen by me—he cut a few strategic slits in the peel, turned it inside out so the white part was showing and positioned the wedge between his front teeth and upper lip. When I happened to glance to my left, Kelly nearly startled me out of the booth with what appeared to be the biggest set of buck teeth I'd ever laid eyes on. Under the best of circumstances, it's hard for me to concentrate on economics and finances. But now that a semi-grown man with a huge, citrus overbite had entered into our conversation, my mind lost any shred of pertinent information Jim and Terry had imparted thus far.

Not to worry, I told myself. *Hadn't I just been invited to that banker's convention? Shouldn't that count for some measure of financial adeptness?*

I assured Jim and Terry that I had the gist of the idea and that all would be fine.

"After all, guys," I asked with a laugh, "how can I mess up a three-minute talk? Besides, I'm getting more and more comfortable in front of groups these days. Just make me a couple of transparencies with all the vital facts and numbers. We can meet before the banquet and run over the figures once more before I get up to speak. The overhead will be a big help."

That evening I arrived early at the Community Center (where the banquet was being held) and saw that the Young Life crew was already in full swing. Poor Jim was so busy putting out fires, coordinating caterers, and practicing with the music and drama team that I could see we were going to have to pitch the idea of practicing the pitch.

It'll be fine, I soothed myself once again. *If I'm anything, I'm a professional.* Somewhere another voice in my head shot back, *Yeah, but a professional* what? So I prayed fervently to come off as a professional pitcher—a professional financial pitcher, that is.

The guests arrived, and we all sat down at paper-covered metal tables to eat our paper-tasting banquet food off of stiff paper plates. Somehow during the dinner I managed to drop a piece of strawberry cake on a transparency Jim had hurriedly given me before the guests started pouring in. I wiped at the smear with my napkin, thinking it really wasn't all that noticeable. It was then, for the first time, that I got a good look at what was to be my visual aid. It was a page of tiny numbers arranged in columns. I panicked as I realized I had no idea what any of them meant or what a ditzy girl like me was doing in a place like this. But it was too late; the show had to go on.

The Young Life gang did a marvelous job: the skits were

A View from the Porch Swing

hilarious, the songs were upbeat and inspiring, and the special speaker delivered one of the most touching messages I'd ever heard about God's unconditional love! Now all I had to do was close us out. Tie up the bow. Give the invitation to make Young Life Greenville's dreams a firm reality.

On my way up to the podium I tripped on the stage. When I got to the mic, it was towering above me like some awkward giraffe. I could not figure out how to lower it, so I bent the flexible, metal neck in a sort of upside down "U" shape and talked up into the metal piece. "There," I said, as my own voice, echoing louder than I anticipated, made me jump. Realizing I could not spend the whole evening with my neck straining up like a small child trying to reach a fountain, I patted the microphone contraption into more of an "S" and finished my sentence. "There now. Here we go."

I began by sharing a heartfelt testimony of what Young Life had meant to me as a teenager, piggybacking off the wonderful message that had just been given. So far so good. But then, the time came where I had to flip the overhead up onto the screen and explain the ministry's current financial situation and projected needs. Do you know how *huge* an otherwise inconspicuous cake smear looks when it is projected onto a banquet hall wall? Believe me, a six-foot cake smear is something to be reckoned with. There was nothing I could do but explain its presence.

Things began going downhill from there, with me stammering and pitifully trying to explain what those little figures meant, tossing out financial-sounding phrases I'd heard as I went along. Mutual fun. Crediting debits. It was not convincing. Imagine Lucy Ricardo from one of the classic "I want to be in Ricky's act" episodes; one of those shows in which she thinks she could ballet with the best of 'em only to realize, too late, that she's in over her head and now her only hope is to escape, leaving as little damage behind as possible.

"This is just the sort of disaster that can happen," my Eeyore-like husband often warns, "with overly optimistic people."

Actually, if I had to pick an old television icon that best described how I sounded by the time I got to the smeared overhead, it probably would have been Mary Tyler Moore from the old *Dick Van Dyke Show*. Remember how Laura's voice would quiver when she had to explain why she was in such a bind?

I remember saying, "Well, um, I think what this, um, basically *means*, is that um, i-i-if you have, say, a whole lot of money, well, um, y-you should—*probably*, I mean I *think*—you should give a whole l-l-lot of money. And i-i-if you don't have very much money, th-then you should put some quarters in a F-Folger's can and save it until y-you have a bunch. I th-think. Ooooh, R-r-r-o-b!"

Only I didn't call for Rob, I called for Jim—who had very much wanted to stay out of the financial pitching limelight this evening. He tried his best to save me, but in the end we just sort of did our best to patch up and close out the night. However, I did a really professional job, I must say, of explaining how to tear off the "commitment section" from the brochure, drawing on my experience as a first-grade teacher. I'm not sure, but I think I also closed us in prayer. I know I prayed for it all to come to a close. Afterwards I found Scott's arms and fell into them laughing and crying at the same time. Somewhere behind me I heard a woman say, "She's so cute." And another set of women said, "That's exactly the kind of financial explanation I've always wanted to hear at these things." But this was one time I really didn't want to be cute. I wanted to be savvy. Or smooth. Or spiritual. Anything but silly. Too much was at stake.

Once we got home, Scott, my reserved husband, who almost never laughs out loud, fell onto the bed in a fit of hysterics. Wouldn't you know, it would be my *disaster* that tickled his funny bone. "Oh, Becky that was *sooo* awful! Do you know how awful that was? I mean [hee-hee] it was so awful that it was the most hilarious thing I've ever seen. It was like a skit from *Saturday Night Live* or something."

I started to cry and through my tears said, "But I didn't mean to be funny this time! This was serious—an important ministry is in the balance here!" but then I found myself laughing hysterically, along with Scott, through my tears. Just about the time we'd both stop laughing and rolling on the floor, Scott would come up for air and repeat, "Oh, that was just *awful,*" and we'd be off holding our stomachs and laughing again. When I finally calmed down, I called Jim's answering machine and left a lengthy message of apology for my first, and last, speech on the economics of ministry.

For the next few days after my nosedive, I received a series of notes and phone calls that were interesting to analyze. They were meant to be thank-you notes and "we appreciate your participation" phone calls, but invariably they all ended up sounding more like humorous sympathy cards. Jim's consolation at church the following week was only semicomforting.

"Becky," he said, patting me on the back, "now I don't want you to worry about it one more minute. Do you really think you could have said or done *anything* that could undo that great message the speaker gave?" I smiled and nodded while inside I thought, *Wow. I was that bad?* Reading between the lines, I interpreted Jim to say, "Becky, just make sure that whenever you speak in public, the speaker before you is *so* good that no matter what you do or say, they will only remember Speaker #1." For some reason this was not making me feel better.

The day after Jim's comment, I was driving down an exit ramp off of Interstate 30 when I witnessed a two-car collision. It looked as though the drivers were OK but there was some serious fender bending. Wanting to be a good citizen (actually wanting to be a good *anything*), I pulled off at the next convenience store and dialed 9-1-1. The operator picked up.

"Yes, Operator," I said breathlessly into the pay phone receiver, "I just witnessed a small wreck on the exit ramp. . . ," I poured it all out at once—the location, a detailed description of the vehicles involved, extent of injuries, my name and phone number. Finally, when I ran out of steam, the operator spoke up.

"Ma'am?"

"Yes?"

"What number did you dial?"

"9-1-1!"

"I'm sorry. You dialed 1-4-1-1. This is information, may I connect you to 9-1-1?"

That does it, I thought. *Is this Becky-Fails-at-Everything Week?* I've seen news stories where *toddlers in diapers* save the day by dialing 9-1-1. I'd been formally introduced to a *cat* that found a way to *paw* 9-1-1! Three little numbers was all I had to remember. I even botched being a good citizen.

The next awful thing I did that very same week involved Kelly (the guy with the lemon-peel teeth), a prized book, and a nutty airline company. Rather than go into detail, I'll just let you read an excerpt of the following letter, faxed in desperation to Herb Kelleher, CEO of Southwest Airlines:

> Southwest Airlines Co.
> Chairman of the Board
> Herb Kelleher
> President & Chief Executive Officer
> Love Field
> Dallas, Tx.
>
> Dear Herb:
>
> Help!!!!!!!!
>
> Let me back up. Southwest has an employee, a flight attendant named Kelly Gaudreau who was presi-

dent of his graduating class. There could not be a more enthusiastic cheerleader of Southwest and Herb Kelleher than Kelly. Not long ago, my son and I ran into Kelly at a restaurant and he insisted that we come over afterwards so he could give us an airplane model and show me a special Southwest employee video and show me his cherished copy of your new book, *Nuts*—a special edition personally signed by you and your assistant, Colleen.

Well, I'm a humorous writer and speaker (I have to do something with all the disasters I get myself into). I opened the back of your book, *Nuts,* and found my Uncle James listed there. He was the arm wrestling champion of the State of Texas (the 61-year-old guy) who took your place at the famous Malice in Dallas Event. *Great,* I thought, *this would be a cute fact to toss into my talk about coming from a colorful family.*

So I asked Kelly if I could borrow his book, promising to take extra good care of it. (I even took the cover off so it wouldn't get creased.)

Then today, I looked outside at the porch swing where I usually read and yelled, "NOOO, Oh, God, please NO!" Because there, all soaked and bleeding and ruffled from last night's rain storm, was Kelly's prized possession: His *Nuts,* gone!

It is at this point that I'd like to begin my official begging for special dispensation and ask you to sign another copy of a book (if I buy it and bring it to your office? on my knees?) that I can give to Kelly. I just can't face him with this.

Look Herb, you seem like a nice guy. And I'm just having an all round bad week.

Please, please, oh, pretty, pretty please sign a copy of *Nuts* for Kelly to replace the one I ruined and you'd have a fan for life. I'm an author too. (Though not a CEO of an airline or anything. Actually I'm not even a real good airline *passenger.*) I know what a hassle this signing thing can be, but there are special cases . . . and believe me, this qualifies.

Love and Laughter (with fingers crossed),

Becky Freeman

Now if you were Herb, wouldn't you have pity on me? Unfortunately, according to the polite and professional public relations person at Southwest, they are all out of the special edition copies, and Herb isn't signing anymore. Most of the employees didn't even get one. (If he signs one, he has to sign thousands.) "But," she said perkily, "we so enjoyed your humorous letter."

Look, I felt like shouting, *I don't want applause here for writing a cute letter. I want mercy!! I want a new book, and I want it signed by Herb. H-e-r-b. Four little letters. How hard can that be???*

Ah, well. I guess this is just one of those cases where my lack of planning and stupidity does not constitute an emergency for a busy airline president. (Herb, if you're reading this, I still think you are a nice guy. And I understand policy is policy. But let's face it—you really missed a chance to come out the hero in this chapter.)

By the end of this week, I was *not* feeling good about myself.

The End

"What???" you say. "That's all? That's the end?" Where's the sunny little saying, the silvery lining, the happy story that makes you suddenly feel on top of the world again? Where's the jubilee? The porch swing moment?

Sorry.

The only porch swing scene in *this* chapter is the one where I discovered that big, ruffled soaked *Nuts* book. But knowing human nature, I know that sometimes the best thing we can say to another person to cheer them up is, "Man, did I ever blow it— *big time*—this week." Now, you see, you can compare your week to mine and close the book right here feeling infinitely better about yourself. Be my guest.

Actually, something did happen near the end of this week that helped me put my life back in perspective. It involved my youngest son.

And a gun.

(On second thought, maybe you shouldn't close the book yet.)

My soul is downcast within me;
therefore I will remember you.
(Ps. 42:5)

chapter ten
RELAXING WITH OUR FAULTS

I was washing dishes at the kitchen sink when suddenly I heard something hit glass. Whirling around, I saw one tiny, round hole in our living room window, then watched in disbelief as the huge eight-by-four-foot window cracked into a thousand pieces. Through this odd mosaic of glass, I saw Gabe had fallen to the ground outside.

I rushed out the door when, suddenly, he stood up, stared at the window in shock, threw his BB gun down on the ground, and ran around the house holding his hands over his eyes—as if by doing so he could shut out what had happened. I found him several minutes later on his big brother's bed, hidden under the covers, convulsed in tears.

"Gabe, Gabe," I said soothingly as I sat down near the lump on the bed. "It's going to be OK. Are you all right?"

"No!" he shouted, never one to stuff his feelings. Between sobs and from under the covers he cried, "I tripped, and the gun fired up instead of down. I want to be invisible! I want to be in another country. I don't know what to do. I can't face Daddy! He just finished building that pretty room! Will you take me somewhere far away? I can live somewhere else!"

"Oh, Gabe," I said, holding his blanketed, mummified form and rubbing what I guessed to be his back. "Accidents happen. All of us blow it sometimes. Think of all the stupid things I did this week. Remember how I left that important book out in the rain? And just last week your daddy slammed into the front door with his back, trying to move in a piece of equipment, and he shattered the glass in it! Daddy won't be upset—he knows how bad you feel already. I'll go get him and explain what happened. You'll see what I mean."

I left to find Scott and plead Gabe's case. I quickly informed him of the mishap, and within minutes Scott had taken my place there on the bed beside his distraught son. As I passed by the bedroom I saw Scott holding Gabe in his arms, stroking his dark hair, telling stories of all the baseballs he'd thrown through windows when he was a kid.

"Son, it's just something ten-year-old boys do at least once in their lives. You'll be more careful from now on. We're just glad you aren't hurt. Glass can be replaced; people can't." Gabe fell asleep within minutes, totally exhausted from his ordeal of self-flagellation.

Observing Gabe's trauma I wondered, *Have I really changed all that much since I was a child? Aren't I more like a ten-year-old than I want to admit when it comes to making mistakes—punishing myself mentally over and over again for not being perfect? And all along, my Father is there beside me, holding out comfort, saying,*

"Becky, did you forget again? You don't have to be perfect. You don't even have to be all that good at anything. Just be yourself. I forgave you long ago, so forgive yourself—and let me rock you and hold you and love you when you blow it. Then get back up and go after it again. I'll be here whenever you need me."

Charles Spurgeon once said, "The strong are not always vigorous, the wise not always ready, the brave not always courageous, and the joyous not always happy." We can't let our mistakes or temporary downtimes or even our lapses into sin define who we really are. We may be *acting* weak, depressed, and immature. Who we *are* is what God sees, because what God sees when He looks at our hearts is Jesus.

I no longer live, but Christ lives in me (Gal. 2:20a).

Do you ever get in one of those head-bowed, "please-don't-hit-me" attitudes toward God? It's a feeling that says, "I'm not living up to His standards, so He's probably mad at me, or at the very least, wants something from me." I read a quote by C. S. Lewis once—a story his wife related to him that she found enormously comforting for times like this. So comforting in fact, that I typed it out and filed it under "Thoughts That Make My Neck Muscles Unwind."

Lewis wrote, "Joy tells me that once, years ago, she was haunted one morning by a feeling that God wanted something of her, a persistent pressure like the nag of a neglected duty and till mid-morning she kept on wondering what it was. But the moment she stopped worrying, the answer came through as plain as a spoken voice. It was, 'I don't want you to do anything. I want to give you something' and immediately her heart was full of peace and delight."

The life I live in the body, I live by faith in the Son of God, who loved me and gave himself for me (Gal. 2:20b).

My sister, Rachel, and I have burned up the phone line between us this past year as we've shared our struggles to give up "performing," and we're finding new contentment in simply re-laxing as daughters of a loving Father. Our midlife battles have in-cluded overcoming disillusionment with God, motherhood, mar-riage, our shortcomings, and life in general. Now, as we are both coming out of our own tunnels, we're catching brilliant glimpses of light—light that comes from accepting ourselves, flawed as we are, and clinging to the reality of God's grace. Recently, Rachel sent me a page from a book called *The Joy of Imperfection*. I smiled at the list of affirmations placed at the end of one of the chapters:

I fondly accept my imperfections.
I have fabulous flaws.
My flaws make me unique and therefore priceless.
Love me; love my flaws.
I am greater than any one part of me.
I'm always a partial success.
I'm totally lovable, even though he, she, or they don't love me.
I'm flawed, therefore I am.

Relax. God made us—flaws and all. He's not out to get us. On the contrary, He's out to give us something: the unconditional love of a Parent for a child—even a child who messes up a lot.

Have you ever watched a toddler in a desperate struggle to put toothpaste—that he's just squirted all over the bathroom—back into the tube? How vividly I remember quietly watching my child from the doorway, chuckling to myself, waiting for him to turn helpless chubby hands up to me, offering an "uh-oh" grin in my direction. So, too, I believe our heavenly Father often shakes His head and sometimes even smiles as we struggle to fix the unfix-able by ourselves. He patiently waits until we've exhausted our-selves and finally offer the mess we've made of our lives up to Him. He waits for us to poke our heads out of the covers long enough to let Him render aid and comfort.

He doesn't want anything *from* you.

He wants to *give* something to you: the compassion of a Dad who understands we are kids.

*The L*ORD* is compassionate and gracious,*
slow to anger, abounding in love. . . .
As a father has compassion on his children,
*so the L*ORD* has compassion on those who fear him;*
for he knows how we are formed, he remembers that we are dust.
(Ps. 103:8, 13–14)

chapter eleven

DIPPING INTO ECSTASY

There's an old Chinese saying I love: "After ecstasy, the laundry."

Isn't that the truth? There's a time for ecstatic, incredible, magnificent experiences, and then there's a time for pouring detergent into a tub full of dirty socks. Funny how we seem to need both to stay balanced.

Our second son, Zeke, is affectionately known as the "spiritual" one in our family. That is, he's been blessed with a tender heart, a peace-loving nature, and an insatiable curiosity about the things of God. He also lives for adventure—constantly planning and executing huge events like evangelistic outdoor concerts or backpacking/rock climbing/water rafting/parachuting/bungee-jumping class field trips.

He's only fifteen; no telling what we're in for in coming years.

Zeke's the kind of guy who revels in life's ecstatic mountain-top moments. So it's tough, sometimes, when Scott and I have to remind this wonder child that there's a pile of laundry waiting at the bottom of Thrill Hill.

I remember one morning in particular when Scott needed Zeke to help him move some lumber from the truck to the upstairs loft. He looked everywhere for the boy to no avail until finally he spotted Zeke sitting near the rippling lake at sunset, an open Bible in his lap. He was contentedly munching on an apple, a faraway look in his eyes.

"Well, there you are!" Scott blurted in exasperation. "Look, Son, I love you, and I'm really glad you're so deep and all. But there's a time to pray, and there's a time to move lumber. Right now you need to move lumber." After ecstasy, the lumber.

For most grown-ups I know, however, the imbalance in our lives is not a result of too little laundry. (I haven't seen the bottom of the clothes hamper in fifteen years.) Imbalance for most of us in our busy world is more likely to come from a shortage of ecstasy—which I define as an overwhelming, heart-lifting, yes, *emotional* response to God and all the large and small blessings He gives us to enjoy.

Now I'm not suggesting we live our life or make decisions based solely on feelings. I once heard James Dobson on the radio discussing the title of his book, *Emotions: Can You Trust Them?* "I basically took a whole book," Dobson quipped, "to say, 'No, you can't.'" What I *am* crying out for is balance. There's every good reason to squeeze all the joy out of the experiences God graciously grants us. I view this as the chocolate glaze on my otherwise plain-pound-cake days. Why eat plain cake when, with a little extra effort, it's possible to enjoy a gourmet delight? It's laundry hung in sunshine, duty dipped in joy. And I believe that by purposely incorporating certain activities into our lives we can experience more jubilees of the heart.

I grew up in a Bible church where the intellect seemed somehow elevated as a superior part of man's psyche, and I believe many of us with similar church roots may have missed just how deeply God desires to nourish and care for our emotions, as well as our mind and soul. We're top-heavy. Our heads are full; we know our apologetics and our hermeneutics. If the truth be known, however, our hearts are often found wanting—a common bane for left-brained, studious people. That's why we need all parts working together—fact *and* feeling—both in our own bodies, but also in the larger body of Christ.

A musician, Chuck Girard, came to our church this past weekend. He, as many of you may remember, was one of the founders of Christian contemporary music. Back in the early seventies, Chuck Girard was a member of the California-based musical group Love Song, famous for songs like "Two Hands," "Little Country Church," and "Little Pilgrim." Their folk-style lyrics brought thousands of flower children and hippies streaming—in their bare feet—to Jesus, thus helping to create that exciting, wonderful, innocent, turbulent period known as the Jesus Movement.

I'm pleased to report that Mr. Girard has grown up nicely. He's wise, mature, gentle-natured, spiritually sensitive, and amazingly talented. He still has the famous red beard, though now it's neatly trimmed. (He said a little old lady once told him, "Son, I'm sure glad Jesus cleaned you up on the inside. Now I can't wait until He cleans you up on the outside.") Chuck was real and relaxed, teaching the seminar in jeans and sneakers, and catching us up on his ministry now. He's alternating between being a family man (he has two grandbabies!), writing and recording songs (under his own label), and ministering to churches worldwide, teaching them about the value and power of worship.

Someone in our church had seen Chuck's web page and invited him to come share with us, neglecting to inform him that our church, for the most part, is not of a charismatic persuasion. So when Chuck first began to speak to us, things were a little touch-and-go. Every time he casually mentioned "healing" or "tongues" or "words from God" the cringing and grinding of teeth from much of the audience was palpable. I was afraid he was about to become Bible church bait.

When Chuck realized what was happening, he stopped and with all sincerity said, "Look, I don't know exactly where you guys are coming from, but the last thing I want to do is stir up conflict or dwell on dividing issues. I just came to offer what I'm learning about how to enter in to worship."

Then he stepped to the keyboard, closed his eyes, prayed, and began playing and singing softly. "Sometimes Alleluia." "Slow Down." "As the Deer Pants for Water, So My Soul Cries for Thee."

That's when something strangely wonderful began to happen.

All of us, from the Conservative-Theological-Seminary-Trained Bunch to the All-Gifts-Are-for-Today Group to what I call the Somewhere-in-Betweeners were ushered into the presence of God on melodies of praise. Softly, quietly, "all in one accord," we worshiped our King with all of our hearts and souls.

We came away from the weekend changed—as individuals and as a church body. Though our heads still held many different views and interpretations of Scripture, we felt our hearts melting together during the times we sang, prayed, worshiped, and adored our mutual Abba-Father, our Lord and King. I couldn't help but think of Jesus' prayer in John 17, "My prayer for all of them is that they will be of one heart and mind, just as you and I are, Father."

It was an emotional experience. Healing. Unifying. Vital and valid.

Who can honestly examine the Scriptures from start to finish and not see a God rich in the full range of emotions? From devastation to ecstasy, His expressions of love, anger, hurt, jealousy, mercy, and, yes, *passion* fairly pulsate from the pages.

Whenever I think of the word *passion* I think of my friend Roz. As you might suspect from someone with a name like Roz—she's unique. A redheaded spitfire who found love late in life (with a man fifteen years her junior!), Roz lives life to the absolute hilt, relishing every moment. People genuinely fascinate her. She wrote a book and named it, appropriately, *Passion!,* and in it she wrote a remarkable sentence I can't get out of my head: "Instead of grabbing life with their bare hands and relishing it, people seem to be handling it with tongs."

It's time to push up our shirtsleeves. In the next few chapters we'll be putting the tongs aside and digging into life with bare hands.

For now, the laundry can sit and soak.

Ecstasy awaits.

Heart, body, and soul are filled with joy. You have let me experience the joys of life and the exquisite pleasures of your own eternal presence.

(Ps. 16:9, 11, TLB)

chapter twelve
READING FOR YOUR HEART

I laughed out loud in empathy at a sign written in scroll across the top of the bookstore's shelves. "When I get a little money I buy books and if any is left I buy food and clothes." The quote was attributed to Erasmus, but I could have said it myself. I, too, am a confirmed bookaholic.

I could stay happily locked up—for weeks—in a well-stocked library. As a matter of fact, if I had my dream vacation it would be a seaside resort, perfect weather, and a blank check to Barnes & Noble.

There are so many wonderful things waiting to be discovered. No matter how tightly packed my schedule, I always seem to squeeze in enough time to read (or at least to skim) two to three books a week. A day without reading? Are you kidding?! You may as well ask me not to breathe.

What do I read? I love to laugh and much of my writing comes from my own scatterbrained, comical life. But most of my reading is serious in nature, contemplative and informative: theology, philosophy, psychology, oncology. Real human beings, especially, and how we relate to one another, to life, and to God holds unending fascination for me.

I think this hunger for knowledge may have been inherited from my Granddaddy Jones. Granddaddy lived at poverty level most of his life in an old broken-down house brushed gray and red with West Texas sand. I now realize he was somewhat of an eccentric, though I saw nothing unusual about Granddaddy when I was a child. He always wore the same thing: beige work coveralls and a hat. He smelled of hand-rolled cigarettes, sweat, All Bran and prune juice. He'd often tape messages to things around the house to let us kids know what could and could not be touched. Across a jar of his favorite pear preserves he wrote, "For my own personal use." But I thought he was wise, inventive, and completely wonderful. He thumb-tacked my school picture—the one with my headband falling off and a couple of front teeth missing—right at kid's eye-level, smack in the middle of the kitchen wall. I loved him for that.

I remember going out to Granddaddy's barn (where he spent most of his days) and standing in complete awe of his surroundings. Everywhere the eye could see there were stacks upon stacks of books. There were so many in fact, they made thick maze-like walls, towering high above my head. In the center of this barn of books was an old, overstuffed chair, a lamp, and a pen—which Granddaddy used to underline passages he agreed with or scribble a silent protest.

It's encouraging to read that scientists are now discovering so many benefits of keeping an active mind. For example, when we exercise our brain by learning lots of new things, did you know the synapses in our brain cells actually become more efficient? (No matter our age!) When we tackle something outside of our comfort zone of knowledge—let's say a computer nerd learns to play the violin—the neurons really go crazy, branching wildly. Learning something new every day, keeping the mind active into old age, is now thought to delay the onset of senility and slow the progression of Alzheimer's disease.

With all the talk about exercise and controlling cholesterol, it's a little known fact that "a major study found that the number of years in education is a more important factor in determining risk of heart disease than all the other risk factors combined!" (So I'm wondering—does this mean I can lay around on the couch and eat bon-bons all day and still be healthy—as long as I'm reading *War and Peace?*)

Of all the reading I love to do, there's one book I've never outgrown. Like the pot of oil that fills up every time some is taken away—God's Word gets richer and deeper the more I read it. How many insights are there in those pages, as yet undiscovered? Even as I reread the most familiar stories—the ones I've heard since childhood—new truths begin to surface. The Bible represents, to me, the ultimate treasure hunt, and I love to go digging into its verses to see what precious gem I might uncover today.

Someday, when we retire, I want Scott to build my own private Book Barn just like my Granddaddy Jones's. There I'll sit all day as I read to my healthy heart's content—with one minor adjustment: I want my barn to come fully equipped with indoor and outdoor porch swings.

"God gave them knowledge and skill in all literature and wisdom."
(Dan. 1:17, NKJV)

chapter thirteen
SOAKING UP NATURE

It is the end of February, and we've had several seemingly un-ending days of rain—setting a new county record of "yuck." These are not the days of fresh, spring showers but ones of dull, gray-brown, cloudy days of wintry-cold rain. People everywhere—at the gas station, restaurants, the kids' school, in the neighbor-hood—talk of little else but our mutual starvation. Our eyes have a gnawing hunger for light—the bright, sunshiny kind. The kind folk singers croon about—warming our shoulders, making us happy. And we can't wait for our first taste of the brilliant, green leaves, which we know are hidden somewhere in those colorless, dripping branches. We long for nature's palette of beauty—one of the richest sources of feel-good joy in life. Who knows how many psalms, hymns, songs, and poems have been inspired by the sight of a mere leaf or blade of grass, much less a magnificent mountain range, a waterfall, or ocean waves?

To tide me over until I can soak up something alive and green, I've enjoyed watching some rented movies set in lush, green English countrysides or exotic forest locales. A temporary fix, I'll grant you, but nonetheless helpful. These days I'll take what I can get—even virtual beauty.

According to the book *Healthy Pleasures,* "we have an appetite for such visual feasts." More than a luxury, research shows that "flooding our brains with rich natural visual stimulation helps us recover from surgery, tolerate pain, manage stress, and attain well-being." Not only that, but people the world over seem to have the same sort of response to beautiful, natural scenes. "When people view slides of natural scenes, they report much higher levels of positive feelings, such as friendliness and elation, and reduced feelings of sadness and fear than do people looking at man-made, urban scenes."

Doesn't this make you wonder if we are going about the urban/violence crisis all wrong? Perhaps we don't need more police or gun control or special after-school programs. Maybe all we need to do is to haul truckloads of dirt and manure filled with grass seed to the downtown ghettos. Follow that up with a few cows, ducks, and pigs, hang a porch swing on every stoop, and—voilà—instant friendliness and elation. Urban Jubilee. I don't know why the government doesn't consult me on these things.

Thankfully, we can count on the world turning pretty and velvety when the sun goes down, no matter what season it happens to be. My husband, Scott, loves to go out walking—yes, after midnight. In the moonlight. Even in February. It's earned him the nickname "Moonwalker."

On summer evenings, Scott's even been known to sneak out of the house at night, quietly row out the bass boat to the middle of the lake, stare up at the sky full of stars, and, if the water is nice, dive in for a refreshing dip. (This I can't quite bring myself to do. I've seen a water moccasin or two out there. I've also observed that they are dark in color and blend really well with lake water.)

Because we live in the country, Scott and I often go for strolls together up and down our tar-covered roads, even after dark. There's nothing quite like watching a night sky—whether it be from a boat, on a walk, doing the backstroke over the water, or dangling in safety from the front porch swing—to put one's self back in perspective.

One of my all-time favorite relaxing-in-nature books is Anne Morrow Lindbergh's *Gift from the Sea*. It always brings me, mentally, to a warm, relaxing beach—a great book to read in the dead of winter! If, by chance, you are going to the beach anytime this year, I highly recommend you tuck a copy of this classic into your tote bag to unwind by.

In one chapter, Lindbergh recalls what to her has been a spectacularly perfect day. She and her sister had escaped from their families to vacation together in a small cottage by the sea. They spent the morning and afternoon swimming, chatting, doing small chores, sharing lunch, and then each went her own way to write or read for a few hours. Coming back together again at dusk, Anne describes so beautifully the way Scott and I feel about nighttime:

> Evening is for sharing, for communication. Is it the uninterrupted dark expanse of the night after the bright segmented day, that frees us to each other? Or does the infinite space and infinite darkness dwarf and chill us, turning us to seek small human spark?
> We walk up the beach under the stars. And

when we are tired of walking, we lie flat on the sand under a bowl of stars. We feel stretched, expanded to take in their compass. They pour into us until we are filled with stars, up to the brim.

This is what one thirsts for, I realize, after the smallness of the day, of work, of details, of intimacy—even of communication, one thirsts for the magnitude and universality of a night full of stars.

Or as the psalmist sang on solitary, black nights, with sheep bleating softly in the background: *"When I consider thy heavens, the work of thy fingers, the moon and the stars, which thou hast ordained; What is man, that thou art mindful of him?"* (Ps. 8:3–4, KJV).

God's heaven and earth is waiting to be relished. Spectacular displays, free for the taking, are right outside our front doors.

I marvel at the beauty, not only in God's creation, but also in the intricate detail found in the construction of His Old Testament dwelling place, the temple: gold and silver; scarlet, purple, and blue cloth; jewels of all kinds; handcrafted wood carvings.

The beauty of the earth and the glory of His temple—mere appetizers of the visual feast that awaits us in heaven when we will behold the beauty of God Himself with unveiled face.

And let the beauty of the LORD our God be upon us.
(Ps. 90:17, NKJV)

* * *

It finally came! Today I edit and add these sentences in the full blossom of spring! Sun on my shoulders, breeze in my hair, and green, green, green—as far as the eye can see. Breathtaking. Even my cold toes are beginning to thaw.

Be encouraged, my friend. So many things we struggle with in life, like those dead-looking trees, take a little *time* to blossom into things of beauty. It helps us to relish and appreciate our springs when they finally arrive.

To everything there is a season. . . . He has made everything beautiful in its time.
(Eccles. 3:1, 11, NKJV)

chapter fourteen
BEFRIENDING THE LITTLE ONES

I gave birth to all four of my children at home.

In natural, cozy, excruciating pain.

Which brings me, believe it or not, to one of the most joyful experiences in life.

All of my kids' births were miraculous, but the debut of my daughter was, hands down, the most interesting. Rachel Praise chose to make her grand entrance into the world during one of the coldest winters in the history of the United States. Condensation froze on the windows *inside* the house, and snow and sleet fell in sheets outside our tiny home. My parents and my sister, Rachel (eighteen at the time), were visiting for the holidays, and they all needed to return home. I was overdue and felt like a watched pot waiting to boil. I had already imagined several instances of labor pains about which we had notified our midwife (a good friend by this time), but so far, I had been unable to produce a grandbaby and niece/nephew for my audience. But at about two o'clock in the morning on December 28, I woke Scott to tell him I was in labor.

"Go back to sleep," he yawned. "I don't even think you're pregnant anymore." The interesting thing is, I managed to go back to sleep, but the next time I woke up, there was absolutely no doubt. I was pregnant, but I wouldn't be for long.

The scene that followed was like a Keystone Cops episode. I yelled orders while Scott scrounged in the closet for the box of supplies I had assembled for the midwife. I realized the box was now the "Do-It-Yourself Birth Kit" because the midwife was thirty minutes away in good weather.

Daddy got on the phone to the midwife, relayed messages to Mother, who hollered them to Scott, who was the most qualified at this point to officiate since he had assisted at the first two home births we had hosted. In the meantime, my very together sister took careful notes in the section of her loose-leaf organizer entitled "Things I Must Never Do." Then she dove in to help, ready to boil rags or tear up sheets, though we never figured out what we needed either of those for.

When the baby was born into Scott's waiting arms, he tearfully announced it was another boy. A few seconds later, Mother said, "Scott . . . um . . . I think you are looking at the umbilical cord there." We named her Rachel Praise, meaning "God's innocent lamb of praise."

I told this story in *Worms in My Tea,* but there's more to the story than I was ready to reveal four years ago. When Rachel was born, she was not breathing. I knew from Zach and Zeke's births that babies sometimes need a little time to get their breathing started, but it seemed to all of us that this baby was taking way too long. I've always been a wimp when it comes to emergencies, so to this day I'm amazed at how the mother in me took control. I reached for the suction bulb in our "birth bag," held Rachel's still slick, warm, little body in my quivering arms, and began suctioning out her nose and throat, praying, "Jesus, help my little girl breathe." When she let out that first beautiful gasp, followed by indignant sputters and a husky cry, we all burst into tears with relief.

The midwife finally arrived and officiated over the cutting of the cord. That out of the way, I held my newborn daughter in my arms as Scott, my parents and sister, the midwife, and two groggy big brothers held hands in a ring around us as we offered heartfelt thanks. Rachel Praise was literally christened into this world with prayers of praise.

As every mother and father knows, there are few moments in life that compare to the elation of receiving a child into this world. And it doesn't end with the birth. With little ones around, every day is brand new. They make us see the world through wonder-filled eyes. The excitement of Christmas morning, almost forgotten, comes back again as we watch their eyes sparkle in delight at the sight of multicolored lights glistening on the tree. From doodle-bugs to daisy petals—the mundane turn into objects of marvel. Only a child can point to a dirty oil smear and see the "pretty rainbow" on the driveway.

But how can childless couples, or singles, or those of us who are out of little ones and not yet into grandbabies, reap the benefits of being with children?

Almost every day there are opportunities to receive "one of the least of these" into our hearts. My friend, Sam Meserve, to whom this book is dedicated, never outgrew the nursery—even though he was in his seventies. He and his precious wife, Doris, faithfully rocked babies and soothed toddlers in the church nursery for over four decades. Now that my own children are growing up, I'm more free to look around and enjoy other children. Yesterday as I was shopping in a department store, I found a little three-year-old, brown-eyed beauty bawling her eyes out.

"Sweetie," I asked, kneeling down to her level, "did you lose your Mommy?"

She nodded through her sobs. So I smiled and said, "How about I hold you up high and let you look all around the store, and let's see if you can find her?" She put her chubby arms around my neck, and when I asked, "Do you see her?" my lost little girl spied her mommy. The dimpled smile spreading across her tear-stained cheeks made me laugh aloud. Sometimes I forget how a child's smile can warm an ordinary day.

Children can be a source of joy for all of us, whether we are parents or not. (It's actually sometimes easier when you can take them in small doses.) But often, kids are ignored or shoved off to the side. One of the things I love about my mother and father is the way they treat children—all children. Both of them have a way of making little ones feel welcome in their home. Mother still keeps a closet of baby dolls, games, and cars for children who come to visit with their parents. Though my father is a fairly high-ranking executive in a large corporation, he's just as comfortable chatting with kids about puppy dogs and balloons and rainbows as he is discussing bids in boardrooms.

So even though my kids are growing up fast, I decided during the process of writing my last book, *Still Lickin' the Spoon,* that I'd always have a Welcome Corner for Kids in my house. Tucked into a window seat in our dining room, there are assorted stuffed animals and baby dolls, coloring books and crayons, beads and string, and a bright, wooden watermelon stuffed with children's books. Above it all is a picture of Jesus with children in His lap and pushed in everywhere around Him. It's a small, tangible way of saying, "You little ones are valued in this home, and guess what? You're even more important to Jesus."

BEFRIENDING THE LITTLE ONES

A dear friend of mine whose children are grown has a little five-year-old neighbor boy over once a week to help her make a batch of cookies or write little books or play a game of cards. She's a busy professional, but she sets aside this day for several reasons. For one thing, this little boy saw his baby brother killed last year when the family car rolled over him. He needs all the love he can get right now.

"Becky," my friend says, "I started out doing this as a way to encourage this hurting little boy. But I'm finding that I can't wait for our afternoons together. He brings so much joy and laughter into my life. Everyone needs a five-year-old friend!"

I'm convinced that children are one of the most overlooked sources of fresh insight and joy. If you can befriend a child, you will be blessed. I guarantee it. Perhaps you might want to gather a special children's box to tuck away in the closet or designate a child's play area in your home. (I love looking at mine even when there are no wee visitors in there.) If you are childless at the moment, you might consider offering a porch swing time: Share some lemonade and a book with a child of some weary mother who is in desperate need of a short break. Then get ready to have your life brightened with some kid-style Jubilee.

"Any of you who welcomes a little child like this because you are mine, is welcoming me and caring for me."
(Matt. 18:5, TLB)

chapter fifteen

WORKING WITH A GRIN

My friend Mary loves small children, and don't get me wrong, but she's always loved them in small doses. So you can imagine my surprise when I found out that she'd taken a position this year as a teacher's aide working with preschoolers and kindergarteners.

I could hardly wait until the clock hit 4:00 so I could call Mary and find out how her first day went.

The phone rang several times before Mary picked up. When she finally did, her voice had a tired, ragged edge to it.

"Mary," I asked, "how was the big day?" I hoped I sounded sympathetic, grateful that my wide grin couldn't be seen via the phone line.

"Becky," she answered sleepily, stifling a yawn, "I tell ya, I just don't know if I'm gonna make it or not. I started off chipper enough this morning. I wore a denim jumper and apple earrings and a big bow in my hair—the whole kindergarten uniform. Even figured out how to mimic the 'happy' tone of voice the other teachers were using. But by noon I was already heading downhill."

"What happened?"

"Well, I found this little guy wandering the hall when it was time for our class to go out to recess, and this child was bound and determined to give me a hard time. He kept saying, 'I'm not going outside, Mrs. Johnson.' I was positive that yes, indeedy, he was going outside, and so after several seconds of this verbal tug-of-war I firmly escorted him by the hand out to recess."

"Good for you, Mary," I said with approval. "If you don't establish authority from the first day you'll be struggling with it all year long."

"Yeah, well, that's not the end of the story. A few minutes later outside on the playground, this same little guy comes up to me, tugs on my skirt, and says, 'Teacher, I don't want to be out here.' I was more than exasperated by this time. 'Look,' I told him, 'this is getting really old. *Why* don't you want to be out here?' Then very quietly he answered, ' 'Cause, Mrs. Johnson, I'm not in your class.' "

I laughed and tried to comfort my friend at the same time. "Mary, remember how many mistakes I made that first—and last—year I taught school? Just be sure to write this stuff down. You'll gather some great stories, and you know I'm a vulture for good material."

"So glad I can be of service."

"Want a piece of advice from a retired teacher?"

"Oh, sure, Becky. You retired from teaching after—what?—ten long months of faithful service?"

"Touché. But this is one of the reasons I took early retirement: It was too hard for me to disconnect from 'teacheritus.' You'll see what I mean. You'll get so used to hearing yourself called 'Mrs. Johnson' and using that 'teacher voice' all day that it's hard to switch when you get back home to civilian life. Scott used to get so aggravated at me when I'd forget to change modes and start talking to the family as if they were a class full of six-year-olds. 'Family, we want our living area to be neat and clean, don't we? So let's pick up our socks and shoes for Mrs. Freeman by the count of three, OK? One, two . . . oh, someone doesn't have their listening ears on.' "

"Oh, great. Maybe that'll happen to me, too, but I don't know. By the end of today 'Mrs. Johnson' was not only losing her teacher voice, she was only allowed to have safety scissors. I keep re-peating to myself, 'This job will be just like pregnancy. Nine months and it's over.' "

So went Mary's Day One. In all honesty, I never dreamed she'd make it to Day Five. At this writing, however, Mary is on Day Forty-five, and I don't think I've ever heard her sound happier or more fulfilled in a job. Yesterday she came over for coffee with her blue eyes sparkling as she chatted about a little Spanish-speaking girl who'd just come into the classroom straight from Colombia.

"Becky, it was so neat. The poor thing was crying, scared by all the new surroundings, and *I* was actually able to calm her using my high school Spanish. By the end of the day she was say-ing, 'Me gusto Señora Johnson mucho, mucho, mucho.' "

"Oh, Mary, she did not."

"OK, she didn't. But she will. She will . . ."

Mary's remarkable transformation is just one example of what happens when people fall into work and suddenly realize a mar-velous thing: They are needed. It's why Mother Teresa was able to smile and thrive in the most pitiful of conditions. She knew her life's work had meaning and purpose. "There are no great tasks," she said, "only small tasks done with great love."

Some have termed this phenomenon the "helper's high." Study

after study has shown that people who are in the business of helping others are happier, healthier, and live longer lives. George MacDonald once said, "Nothing makes one feel so strong as a call for help." It's amazing how we rise to occasions when we know our input will make a real difference in others' lives.

Those who see their careers as having a positive impact on people's lives may not always have money, power, or prestige, but they are among the most blessed workers on earth. They have what I like to call On-the-Job-Jubilee.

You've probably heard the true statistic that most heart attacks occur at 9:00 A.M. on Monday morning. Among the fourteen positive factors that retard aging, a happy marriage is number one, with job satisfaction following close behind as number two. That's just one of the reasons it's vital that we occasionally pause and examine our life's work.

Scott and I went to a folk singing festival one day and happened upon a couple named Jim and Suzanne. Jim, wearing a homespun shirt of pale blue, picked out a lively tune on his banjo. Suzanne wore a prairie-style dress in a matching shade and steadily strummed a guitar's strings. Together they were harmonizing to an old western song.

What struck me as peculiar about this old-timey couple is that they were about the same age as Scott and me. And somehow, this thirty-something couple was making a living playing ballads and folk tunes for schools and fairs around the country.

During a break, I asked Suzanne if she had time to put her feet up and chat; she seemed pleased to join us. By this time, I was bursting with curiosity.

"So Suzanne, I've just got to know—why is it that you and your husband are making careers out of singing 'Drifting Along with the Tumbling Tumbleweed' when everyone else in our age group programs computers?"

"Well . . . ," she began with a smile, the metal on the bottom of her laced clogging boots clanking as she shifted in her chair. She swung her long, dark curls behind her back and continued.

". . . I was a college student in Virginia a few years ago, and one day I came across a book of old folk tunes and just fell in love with them—great songs from bygone days when people used to have sing-ins around pianos and campfires and porch swings. I guess they touched a nostalgic nerve in me, and I knew I wanted to find a way to share them with others, especially with children."

"So what you are doing today—relaxing and jamming and singing old songs—is how you make a *living?*" Scott asked incredulously.

By that time Jim had joined our circle. "Well," he drawled, "we certainly don't own much. Our home's a travel trailer. But you know what we have? We have time to enjoy each other's company. And there's nothing like singing to an audience of fascinated kids. It's a good life, all and all."

By the world's definition of success, Jim and Suzanne are not measuring up. Any good businessman will tell you that schoolchildren are not the best-paying audience. And what about the status of a house, nice furniture, cars, and fine clothes? What about prestige? Aren't those things necessary in order to achieve the American dream of happiness?

In a fascinating book called *Why We Do What We Do*, by Edward L. Deci, I was astounded by a study focusing on the mental health of people who set their life goals around one (or all) of the three most popular extrinsic American values: money, fame, and beauty. Interestingly, the researchers discovered that people who aimed for these goals turned out to be mostly unhappy, suffering from a variety of mental distresses. But those who chose careers that emphasized intrinsic values such as meaningful relationships, personal growth, and reaching out to help others lived happy, healthier lives.

Jesus said, "Whoever loses his life for my sake will find it"

(Matt. 10:39). It is in giving that we receive. Receive what? Money? Power? Prestige? No, the best currency we're paid for doing meaningful work is *joy*.

Even a subtle shift in perspective about the work we are *already* doing can make a huge difference in our satisfaction with life. If a full-time homemaker realizes that she's shaping the lives of her children, building a marriage to last a lifetime, and making a haven for others in need of refreshment—that what she does *matters,* and matters significantly—it elevates her work to a new level. Energy and creativity flourish. Wiping noses, having coffee with a girlfriend, taking the kids to the park, even changing diapers becomes an art form—if it's done with love, creativity, and a sense of purpose.

If pumping gas or working behind a counter can be viewed as "encouraging and helping people" rather than simply ticking off hours just to bring home a buck, then "mundane jobs" move to the realm of "meaningful work." When we take pride in doing a job well, no matter how menial it may seem—"doing small tasks with great love"—even mundane household chores can be acts of worship and joy. (I wonder if my kids would like to perform several small acts of worship and joy, with great love, for me this week.)

If we wrote a résumé of Jesus' earthly life, what would it look like? Born in an animal stall, the son of a carpenter, he spent three homeless years in ministry: walking dusty roads, bringing good news, and healing the hurting. His destiny was to die an excruciating death on a cross between two thieves in order to rise again, laugh at death, and invite us to join Him in eternity. The rich, the famous, the beautiful ways to success are most notably absent. And yet was there ever a man more full of wisdom, joy, and peace?

Jesus also helped others catch a vision for how they could help spread His message. As Harry Emerson Fosdick, in *On Being a Real Person,* put it so well, "Jesus kept laying his hand on unlikely people saying, 'You are needed,' and so awakened in them a transforming respect for their own lives."

What creative work has God given you to do? Where is He pointing right now, whispering to your soul saying, "You, my child, are needed *here*"? As a fellow struggler in this area, I urge you to go forth in complete assurance whenever He says, "Follow me."

The path won't always be easy, sometimes it's downright painful, but ultimately it leads to an On-the-Job Jubilee.

And me? Have I found my creative life's work, my jubilee job? Well, that's another story for another chapter.

"I have brought you glory on earth by completing the work you gave me to do."
(John 17:4)

chapter sixteen

THROWING IN THE TOWEL?

Writing that last chapter on the joy of creative and meaningful work was lots of fun. But recently I was faced with the task of personally applying what I'd written—at a point when I was close to calling it quits. (I hate it when I'm convicted by my own writing.) So I'm expanding the topic of creative work to include my personal struggles of late with my chosen career.

This week, I received a small pile of 1099 tax forms that added up to a total of—well, I can't tell you, but let's just say it was not in line with what I'd assumed I'd been worth this year. It was a sobering moment, and, still, if I think about it too much, I can get these little depressing waves—akin to nausea—surging through my emotions.

A View from the Porch Swing

Four years ago, fresh from the New Author's Starting Gate, my mom and I found ourselves in the surprising position of being "best-selling writers." We were told by publishers and agents that having a first book from a couple of no-name women to sell this well was like being struck by lightning. (Only we assumed that what we were experiencing was a lot more fun.)

Four years and four more books later, I have given more than two hundred radio interviews, had my picture taken for the cover of magazines, write a monthly column, and have appeared on a few national television shows. Every week I get letters from readers of my books or columns. I have what most people would deem to be a fulfilling and flourishing writing career. So what's the problem?

Here's the glitch: If I add up the hours I spend at this dream career of mine—the research, writing, and rewriting, and the hours of doing my part in "author publicity"—then deduct the expenses of equipment, postage, office supplies, phone, and travel, I'm putting in as much or more time and earning less than I earned as a first-year teacher. Actually, I'm making less than the school cafeteria lady. Oh, shoot, I may even be making less than the *kids* in the cafeteria line! Bumping into a stark realization like this is somewhat like biting into a chunk of baking soda in what had been, up to this point, a delicious chocolate chip cookie.

Which leads me to the personal Big Question of the Day: Why, for goodness sake, should I continue to write? I need to know clearly why I'm doing what I'm doing, so I plan to sit here and figure this out the only way I know how: I'll write until the answer comes.

In fact, I may have already been given a small glimpse of an answer.

This morning my family awoke to below-freezing conditions—*inside* our house. During the night, a January cold front came in just as the butane went out. Scott—my frontier guy—braved the frigid air and took over the morning's rush. While he helped our well-chilled children off to school, I turned my efforts toward thawing. Once the troops were gone, Scott strolled back into our bedroom and found me sitting upright in our bed, rubbing my hands together over a steaming cup of coffee. During his brief absence, I'd been dressing in assorted layers of turtlenecks, thermal underwear, socks, house shoes, pajamas, and robes—then I'd topped myself with a woolly hat and scarf. Propped up on my shivering lap lay Catherine Marshall's classic book, *To Live Again*.

"Come on, Hon," Scott teased as he scanned the cover, "you aren't *that* bad off!"

Actually, I'd grabbed Ms. Marshall's book because the title so perfectly fit my inner search *du jour*. I needed to find my bearings again, motivation to go on since discovering my thirteen-year-old daughter's baby-sitting business was more solvent than my free-lancing career.

"Scott," I asked, my sad eyes following my husband as he walked to the dresser, "do you realize the paltry amount of income I contribute to this family?"

"Becky, you contribute things to this family that money can't buy."

"Like what?"

"Well, you give us someone to make fun of, for one. Classy outfit ya got on there."

He pulled a pair of gloves out of the drawer and slid them on his hands. "Anyway, painters and actors and writers and stuff are famous for their paltriness. And you need to remember how many income-producing opportunities you've turned down because you wanted to stay close to home until the kids are older."

I hung on to one word Scott said. "So you think of me, then, as an *artist?*" I asked, pronouncing the word "ar-teeest." I rubbed my nose to warm it, pulled the scarf up around my chin, lowered the cap over my eyebrows, and waited expectantly for my husband's response. He took a long, gentle look at me, then shook his head as if struggling to accept that he'd married a fruitcake. A frozen fruitcake, at that. Then he strolled out the door, closing it softly behind him. The only thing that kept me from collapsing in a heap of self-pity was the grin I caught on the side of Scott's face as he took his leave. Unmistakable were the little rows of half parentheses on the side of his mouth—evidence that I at least still amused him.

Just then, the bedroom door opened slightly as Scott poked his head back in and announced, "Harold the Butane Man is here!"

"Great!!" I shouted, already anticipating the luscious, warm air that would soon be wafting again through the vents. Then I remembered something about the Butane Man that brought a fresh deposit of depressing thoughts to my freezing and fragile emotions.

"Scott," I asked, "do you remember that time, about four years ago, when Harold came over to fill our butane tank and I was so excited about *Worms in My Tea* that I ran up to his truck, showed him a copy, and told him I was an author?"

"Oh, yeah. Isn't he the one that told you not to quit your day job?"

"Uh-huh. When I told him, 'It's too late, Harold, I already did,' he looked so stunned." I drew the blankets tightly to my chin and leaned back on the pillow. "Maybe Harold was right. Maybe I should have kept a day job."

"Becky, look—you have a day job. OK, I'll say it: You are an ar-*teest*. A rather paltry breadwinner, I'll grant you, but a *magnificent* arteest. And God's meeting all of our needs, isn't He?"

I gave my husband half a smile as he went outside to greet Harold. *What am I doing?* I silently asked the book in my hand, flipping its pages in search of some comfort. *Should I keep writing in faith or jump track now and get myself a real job with a uni-*

form, benefits, a steady paycheck, hot meals on a plastic tray, and maybe even one of those nifty hair nets thrown in? I was running dangerously low on pep-thoughts.

And the soul of the people became very discouraged on the way.
(Num. 21:4, NKJV)

chapter seventeen

WRITING BACK TO LIFE

I turned to the chapter Catherine Marshall had titled "Work for the Hands to Do." My eyes were drawn to a passage Ms. Marshall had quoted from a book she'd read as a little girl, *Emily of the New Moon*. In the book, a teacher asks Emily (who yearns to be a writer), "Tell me this—if you knew that you would be poor as a church mouse all your life—if you knew you'd never have a line published—would you still go on writing—would you?"

"Of course I would," came Emily's disdainful reply. "Why, I have to write—I can't help it . . . I've just got to."

I can't help it . . . I've just got to. . . . Like Emily, like Catherine Marshall, like most writers who love their work, I did not begin writing with a paycheck in mind. I started writing at age eleven because I simply couldn't help it. My mind would be all in a muddle, my thoughts in knots, and it was through writing that I found I could untangle the knots, lining up the pieces until, eventually, they would take on meaning.

Little about professional writing, however, has been as carefree as those childlike pouring-it-all-out-in-my-diary days. I'll never forget the agonizing months of waiting after Mother and I mailed off our first manuscript to a list of publishers. I won't forget how we'd find an editor's letter glinting in the mailbox, hold it to our hearts, dare to hope, and then watch that hope splatter as we'd read things like: "Dear Mrs. Freeman and Mrs. Arnold, we are sorry . . . but we simply cannot publish books with worms wriggling through the text" or "What a coincidence! We already have six similar projects involving black tea and gray invertebrates" or "This is really funny, but alas, as we both know, you two are nobodies. If you get a big television or radio thing going, give us a call."

During that difficult waiting/rejection period, I happened upon a comforting chapter in Madeleine L'Engle's memoirs, *A Circle of Quiet*. In it L'Engle describes a painful day, her birthday, when she'd received the last in a long series of rejection letters.

> So the rejection on the fortieth birthday seemed an unmistakable command: Stop this foolishness and learn to make cherry pie.
>
> I covered the typewriter in a great gesture of renunciation. Then I walked around and around the room, bawling my head off. . . . Suddenly I stopped, because I realized what my subconscious mind was doing while I was sobbing. My subconscious mind was busy working out a novel about failure.
>
> I uncovered the typewriter. . . .

This is the fate of all destined-to-be writers: We cannot *not* write. (By the way—for Madeleine, the wait finally paid off royally. She went on to win the Newberry Award for *A Wrinkle in Time* and has been prolifically published, with numerous accolades, over the years.)

There is another drawback to writing: It has a sneaky way of taking over your life. Ever the observer, I sometimes long to participate more fully in life's moments without constantly wrestling behind-the-scenes thoughts like, *This is such a special, tender moment. Wonder where I could use it?* or *This entire dinner conversation could be worked into my chapter on . . . .* And I'm always near panic when someone says something adorable or profound and I'm caught without pen and scratch paper.

I had to laugh out loud at Susanne Lipsett's observations on *Surviving a Writer's Life:* "You mean life is more than material for books? There's only one thing to do when you find yourself posing that question: Stand up, walk away from your computer or your writing desk, and plunge your poor, steaming head into a bucket of ice water. Then lie down and let the sun dry you slowly while you think about nothing at all." Often, in order to disconnect from my writing world and phase back into the real one, I've had to physically push myself away from the computer and march my legs out to the porch swing. Once there I'll watch leaves dancing overhead or squirrels fussing over an acorn, allowing the wind to stroke my face until I'm generally calmed and my bogged-up head begins to unclog.

Another thing: Writing is hard work—*really* hard work. If only writing would stretch and exercise my body as it does my mind—and my fingers. I have incredibly strong, lean fingers from all the typing I do. The circumference of my fingers is as tiny as a child's. My posterior, however, is another story. And, no, I shall not discuss its current circumference.

The surprising discovery that writing is hard work eliminates many a would-be player from the game of writing professionally. The spaces along the road to the Published Land are often dotted with disappointment. My mother dreamed of having a book published for years, and if anyone deserved it, she did.

Once, when I was in high school, she wrote a well-crafted book—a tender, dramatic testimony of a reformed prisoner. The whole family rejoiced when it was accepted for publication. Then the day the book was to be printed, the reformed prisoner landed himself back in jail for check writing fraud. My mother, with heart breaking for the man's family and all that might have been, made the painful call to stop the presses. I would see uncanny scenes like this repeat themselves again and again. But ever resilient, Mother would dry her tears and return to faithfully pounding the typewriter. Even though I am her daughter and admittedly prejudiced, she is still one of the most talented writers I know.

So when our dual effort was published, it was more than a simple joy; it was an answer to a lifelong dream. We went on to write one more book together, *Adult Children of Fairly Functional Parents*. That accomplished, Mother announced one day that she'd had her fill. Matter-of-factly and with complete assurance she said, "Becky, writing is hard work. Now that I've done it and know I can do it well, I've decided I'd really rather play. Like the tomcat said after romancing the skunk, 'I believe I've enjoyed 'bout all of this I can stand!'"

And play she has. Gardening, bridge, friends for lunch, trips with Daddy, an Alaskan cruise, gourmet cooking, and baking. Yesterday she E-mailed me with a note that they had bought a lot at a lakeside resort. She's delightedly sampling the whole "Life's Short, Let's Enjoy It" buffet.

My Aunt Etta, who is mother's big sister and the family's first published author, continues to write and teach to this day (at age seventy-plus), but she offers no illusions about the stamina it takes to jump into the writing pool. Often, she opens her writing courses at Texas Tech with this famous analogy: "Writing is easy. You just go to your typewriter and open a vein." The glamour of writing fades quickly when confronted every day with a blank computer screen.

I must also confess that I rarely skip to the computer, bursting to capture my overnight profundities. I take the long way around to actually writing: I make coffee. Check my E-mail. Pour the coffee. Pick lint off the couch. Call a friend. Sip the coffee. Stare at the computer and wish it away. Refill coffee cup. Resign myself to the computer. Worry I'll have nothing of consequence to say, then dive in and write anyway. Once my motor gets cranking, the words finally start to flow. If they don't, I make more coffee.

Even when words are finally on paper, it is only the beginning. "Writing *is* rewriting!!" our collective English teachers declared. Unfortunately, they were absolutely right. There is no shortcut, and every chapter I write, this one included, will undergo at least five to ten rewrites. Even then, it won't be perfect. Improvements can always be made. This is why deadlines are a writer's salvation. Otherwise we'd never declare a piece "finished"—we'd write books that never end. Today, my daughter's teacher told her, "Writing's never done, it's just *due."* How true!

Let me pause for a moment here and add up what I've placed on the writing table thus far: Writing often pays precious little, it is hard work, the dailiness of it is unglamorous, and it is teeming with heartache and rejection. (Not to mention that it broadens certain horizons one does not wish to have broadened.) What other career, other than acting and painting, holds forth such an array of questionable benefits? And more to the point, what is a nice girl like me doing in a profession like this?

I love it.

I love it when I write something I know is good—*really, really* good. So good in fact that I stand back in awe, click my tongue, and am compelled to pat my own self on the back. "Girl," I'll say aloud, "where did that come from? Who poured those words through your mind and composed them so beautifully?" There's the fleeting impression every so often that writing is something beyond myself, that perhaps it truly is a gift from above. I also know that a gift, if kept wrapped and stored in some dusty corner, is never fully enjoyed. It must be taken out to the light, unwrapped, and shared. Even if some reject it or don't like its texture or color or style, it still needs to be offered up.

The joy that comes when your written words are not only received, but appreciated, is near to the joy of birthing a child. I keep every note of encouragement—they are megavitamins for days like today, tonic for my timid soul. One letter I keep handy says, "There is nothing in this world aside from sleeping and eating that I love so much as laughing—and that is the gift I thank you for. My husband is truly sleep deprived though, as I have read most of *Worms* aloud to him in bed. When I wasn't reading out loud I was laughing myself sick. If he sees another one of your books in the house he may leave me." A recent letter from a male reader said, "I finished *Marriage 9-1-1* in less than 24 hours. Once again you made me laugh and cry."

Another precious note arrived, not long ago, on a day when I needed a writing lift. "Last summer while on vacation I bought my first Becky Freeman book. What a joy! I laughed and cried, sometimes at the same time. Don't stop writing. God has certainly given you a tremendous gift to bless His children with. Keep listening to Him and He will direct your paths." *Don't stop writing. Keep listening to Him. Laughing is a gift I thank you for. God has given you a gift to bless His children with.*

Now I ask you, how many jobs in the world offer benefits like these? What a blessing to know my feeble attempts at conveying a message actually touch the hearts of strangers—people I'd never meet without the printed word?

Then, there is another joy—the joy of passing on the torch. Every week I see or hear of a talented new writer who just needs a little nudge to get going. Several of them are now published. I'm especially good at encouraging new writers because they come to know me "just as I am"—and I honestly think they leave shaking their heads and saying to themselves, "I do believe if ol' Becky can write books, I ought to at least give it a shot!"

A woman in her fifties recently published her first story after hearing me encourage women to "fling worms"—my pet phrase for doing something wild and crazy (such as taking the risk of using our gifts). She wrote a delightful letter, bubbling with the excitement of seeing her byline in print, and ended it by saying, "As I stare at my WP screen and search for worms to fling while chanting 'I think I can, I think I can,' I rejoice in the ways that Our Father continues to bless willing hands committed to His service." Like Catherine Marshall, another soul found meaningful "work for the hands to do" in the act of writing.

I belong to a writing group that meets on a monthly basis. All of us are nurturing mother-types, so we've dubbed our group Hens with Pens. Their friendship has meant as much to me as anything else I've received from writing. This Monday night, we start our first satellite group. (What will we call them—Chicks with Bics?) There's a pastor coming who's writing a terrific suspense novel for teens, a therapist writing on joy beyond pain, a young wife who's almost finished a romantic novel, an engineer working on a science thriller, and another pastor who wants to put his sermons into Bible study form. Such diversity and talent! I'm eager to see each one of them hold a copy of their own published book in their hands.

If it hadn't been for the right nudges at the right time, Mother and I would have never made it. What a privilege to be on the other end of the nudging.

The people I've met and the friendships I've made with authors and editors and publicists has been another unanticipated delight. If I never wrote another word, as a result of this career I'd have made fascinating friendships that will last a lifetime. What price can you put on new friends? (As my charming Mary Engelbreit calendar proclaims, "Old friends is best 'less you can catch a new one that's fit to make an old one out of." I've caught me a heap of new friends these past few years that are more than fit to make old ones out of.)

Why will I keep writing? Because I can't *not* write. Because it would be wrong to keep a God-given gift under wraps. Because I am thrilled every time readers open my gift and let me know it was just what they needed and hoped for. Because there are other talented writers out there who need to be encouraged, whose stories need to be told, whose gifts need to be polished and made ready for giving—and I want to be there to squeal with them when they sell their first story. Because when I am discouraged and don't know if I can keep going, it is other *writers* whose hard-wrought words lift my spirit and remind me that writing is more than a paycheck, sales figures, and best-seller lists.

Writing, especially under pressure to perform, is not always fun. But writing, letting your words run wild and free, can be pure Jubilee. *Everyone* can unwind their mind with this sort of writing. Actually this is the most healing of writing forms: simply allowing our thoughts to flow out and onto paper—thoughts that we may never share with another breathing soul.

My favorite and happiest times of writing are the simplest— days when I take notebook, pen, and Bible out to my porch swing and write what comes to mind as I soak up the sun. It's also nice to snuggle up on the couch with notebook and pen during the cold, winter months, but there's something especially peaceful about writing in the warm out-of-doors. Here's a sample from an old notebook, dated October 1994:

> If ever there was a Norman Rockwell picture, this is it. I lie here in the dock observing Autumn make her gentle descent on lake and woods. Touches of scarlet and gold—early gifts—adorn the foliage. A large crappie somersaults above the lake and disappears in an instant.
>
> Three boys, one fourteen, the others about age eight, move along the shore in excited murmurs.
>
> "Put it here."
>
> "I saw somethin' move."
>
> "Can I hold it now?"
>
> "It" is a net. Apparently it is the lone (therefore highly coveted) net for catching a school of minnows and other unseen lake-dwellers. I peer to see who wields control of the handle. Yes . . . I see there are decided advantages to being the Big Kid.
>
> As the afternoon sun plays about the boys and warms my outstretched legs, I squint my eyes, nearly closing them—but not quite. As I do, there's a hint of timelessness about this whole scene. Everything takes on an other-wordly glow.
>
> If I should die before I wake from the nap I'm about to take on this wooden pier, I could say I left this world satisfied. After all, I've tasted the best of earth's bounty in moments like this.

There, I've done it again. I knew if I just kept writing, the answer would make itself clear. The waves of nausea are subsiding, I can feel myself sitting taller, and I'm feeling more at ease and sure, content that God will care for my needs as I faithfully use the gifts He's given me to share. I've written my way into writing again.

Well, Harold . . . looks like I'm going to put off that day job a little while longer.

Fan into flame the gift of God.
(2 Tim. 1:6)

chapter eighteen
PONDERING THE BIG STUFF

I'm tempted to call this next section "Deep Thoughts—and I Do
Have Them." Occasionally, anyway. For it's impossible to discuss
this powerful source of joy without pondering some mighty big
thoughts.

Have you checked the religious book section lately at a general bookstore? It is flooded with Eastern philosophy mixed up and
presented for today's modern spiritual seeker. Books on spiritual-
ity are one of the fastest-growing genres in the publishing world
today. In many ways, I can understand how people are deceived
into this vast New Age La-La-Land. In preparation for writing this

book I read no less than twenty of the top-selling New Age books by today's popular "spiritual" writers: Deepak Chopra, Barbara D'Angelis, Wayne Dyer, Marianne Williams, etc. On the surface, it looks like they're offering a buffet of spiritual glazed cake. So accepting, so peaceful, so open. But in reality, I found lots of glaze and no cake underneath.

What I love about true Christianity, in a nutshell, is this: It's about a Father's sacrificial love for us, His children. One missing ingredient in most other major religions (as in so many homes today) is a Father. Among the ninety-nine names of God in Islam, there is not a word that means Father. The same is true for Hinduism and Confucianism. In other religions you must work your way to perfection or be reincarnated for enough centuries, and then you might become a god yourself. Aside from the intellectual reasons I believe Christianity to be true, other religions do not meet my deepest emotional needs—to be accepted though grace, just as I am, by a Father in heaven who loves me. Who even lets us call Him "Abba"—the most familiar, easy-for-a-toddler-to-say Hebrew word for Father. Now that's a God I can get my arms around.

In 1997 thirty-nine Americans engaged in mass suicide because they thought it was a viable way to catch a ride on a UFO on the tail of a comet. "How could people buy into these wild ideas?" we ask in amazement. It just shows how desperate humans are to grasp onto something that promises to be more meaningful than the physical world we see. In his solitary hours, the soul of man cries, *There has to be more to life than working our way up some corporate ladder or plodding our way through the years and then returning to dust. There's got to be more joy than this somewhere beyond the stars! Where do I find that joy?*

And you know what? It's a great question. Unfortunately, people asking great questions like this are often susceptible to any nutcase claiming to have "the answer." But how can we reach today's world with the truth of the gospel?

Larry Norman wrote a breakthrough song that helped usher in the seventies' Jesus Movement called "Why Should the Devil Have All the Good Music?" Today, I find myself asking, "Why do all the New Agers appear, to the world at least, to have all the peace and relaxation?" Peacefulness seems to be the great need of the hour in our fast-forward world.

Could we, of the hardworking, flag-waving, no-nonsense conservative Christian Right, be missing much of what Christ offered to the world in terms of peace and rest here on earth?

I can't help but believe there is scriptural food we're not harvesting and using to feed today's hungry lambs. If we're going to be effective in reaching this world, we may have to pause, take a step back, and ask ourselves tough, honest questions like, "How much of my Christian outlook on life is a result of my Westernized, patriotic, Type A upbringing—and how much is *truly* based on the kingdom lifestyle Jesus Christ taught about?" The more I soak up the Gospels, the more I see that the Son of God had much more to say about genuine joy, peace, love, and relaxation than any guru. But because so many of us American Christians aren't experiencing a calmness of our soul on a regular basis, I think we might be glossing over important truths that could feed a country's frazzled emotions.

For a couple of years now, though I've never written it down in book form, I've given a little talk on "The Three Gardens of the Bible and of Life." As I speak on this subject, I note tense faces melting into peaceful smiles, sometimes tears trickling down cheeks as some give knowing nods, and whenever I give this particular talk, my own spirit is always calmed.

For contained in these gardens is food for hungry searchers and frantic saints.

If you can get to one, you may enjoy reading the next three

chapters in a quiet garden setting. For God chose to meet man's most vital "religious needs" in the peace and quiet of a garden.

"Peace I leave with you, My peace I give to you; not as the world gives do I give to you. Let not your heart be troubled, neither let it be afraid."

(John 14:27, NKJV)

chapter nineteen
FINDING JOY IN OUR EDENS

One day as I was thumbing through the Bible, looking for a spot to land, I noticed with interest that three of the greatest dramas in Scripture are placed against the backdrop of a garden. Then I realized something else. These three garden dramas also coincide with the phases all of us go through in our lives.

First there is the Garden of Eden—the garden of fresh joy. It is interesting that Genesis establishes God as the first gardener. Everything else in the world He spoke into existence. But not this particular garden. The Scripture says God planted this one Himself. Didn't even hire out an angel to do the job. Why?

Do you remember way back in kindergarten when you planted a lima bean in a paper cup? You invested your whole heart into that project. Every day you'd run into the classroom, not to see what everyone else's bean was doing, but to check on your own bean. The one *you* planted. When you plant something yourself, you invest your heart into it. God created the whole world, but this little plot of ground that He personally planted—this garden called Eden—is where He invested His heart.

When Scott and I were newlyweds we planted our first garden. At the ripe old ages of seventeen and eighteen, we didn't have a lot of prior farming knowledge between us to draw upon. When it came time to buy our chosen baby plants—tomatoes—Scott and I calculated that we could probably each eat a dozen or so tomatoes by summer's end. So we went right out to the nursery and bought twenty-two tomato plants.

We loved those tomato plants. Adored and rejoiced in every new leaf, every inch of stem. When bugs attacked our precious baby plants, we attacked back, protecting them with a vengeance. Having read in an organic gardening magazine that bugs are repelled by the smell of other smushed bugs, we spent hours sitting amongst the leaves smashing insects onto leaves with our thumbs. That is, until we got the bright idea to whirl up a batch of bugs in a blender with water. Then we squirted our homemade "bug spray" onto the plants.

Apparently it worked, because we had quite the bumper crop. Much to our innocent surprise, we harvested over three hundred tomatoes from our little patch of garden! (This, after we discovered neither one of us had a great affinity for the taste of tomatoes.)

Interestingly, the thing Scott and I loved most about gardening was not the actual eating of the produce. We loved the shop talk. We liked admiring and discussing and strolling through and sitting near our garden. I often imagine how much God must have enjoyed walking in the garden, in the cool of the evening, just visiting with Adam and Eve, checking out the progress of the garden, and rejoicing together in every new leaf, each new inch of stem.

Sometimes life, too, gives us glimpses of Eden on Earth. There are those special, glorious "Eden days"—like the miraculous births of our children—when God seems so near and real. As I've already pointed out, I wouldn't want to give birth every day—but I have to admit that the joy I felt when I first held my newborns was the closest thing to ecstasy I've ever experienced. Or there are those tender, romantic moments. Perhaps an anniversary. When your husband looks at you tenderly across a candlelit dinner, tells you he loves you more today than ever, then takes your hand and places a tiny, velvet box in your palm. (Inwardly you breathe a sigh of relief because at least you are pretty sure it's not a blender.) Or standing at the edge of the Grand Canyon and watching the sun set in glorious display. These are life's Big Eden Moments.

Those sorts of moments don't happen very often in an average lifetime. But every day there are small glimpses of Eden waiting to be savored. The sun warm on your face, the laughter of a child, the satisfaction of reading a good book under a cozy quilt, coming across a Scripture and suddenly experiencing that deep "knowing" of God's personal love for us.

How do we catch these Eden joys on the wing? It's similar to what we do when we take that famous first sip of morning coffee. Most of us, without even realizing it, comment on the first taste of java. It may be a quiet "Mmmm" or a more verbal "Man, that's good stuff," but we usually pause for a second and acknowledge its goodness. In doing so, like the coffee commercial says, "We celebrate the moments of our lives."

God even had His own variation of this "coffee routine." After every phase of creation, He took time to stop, pause, and notice its goodness. "God saw that it was good."

When I was a kid I would never throw away my gum until I'd "chewed all the *goody* out of it." And so it is with Eden joys. To get the most out of these wonder-filled times—both large and small pleasures—we need to practice squeezing the goody out of life by stopping, pausing, noticing, and breathing a prayer of thankfulness for this moment, right now, that is filled with His goodness.

In her book, *Everyday Sacred,* Sue Bender writes, "Mine is a racehorse rhythm, and once I get started in the morning it's difficult for me to stop. Now I can see that a pause—even a very *small pause*—is extremely useful. These 'little Sabbaths' replenish my body—and spirit." How I identify with this. If I do not pause somewhere near the beginning of my day (usually with or right after that first cup of coffee) and offer a prayer of thanks, I miss my little bit of Eden all day long.

My back porch in the warm spring and early fall is my chosen Eden spot. In winter it's a rocking chair and quilt; in summertime it's the dock, where I can dangle my feet in the water.

I have a friend who moved to the city and was so lonely for her childhood mountain home that she created her own Eden place in her fenced backyard. She bought—yes, *purchased*—a big boulder, then she planted flowers and tree saplings around it and, finally, set a lawn chair in the midst of it all.

"I love my rock," she said fondly, as she proudly showed off her special place. "It was, once upon a time, a part of a mountain." If you don't have an Eden place on hand, you can always make one to your liking.

One last thought before moving on: Eden is a point in our lives to love and savor. No, it may not last forever. Tough times will come; there are other difficult gardens ahead. But when you get to experience even a very small taste of Eden, don't waste the lovely present by dreading imagined and dismal futures. Enjoy what you have right now to the hilt.

I feel sorry for newlyweds who get all sorts of well-meaning warnings of hard times to come—at a time when the young lovers are smack in the middle of their Eden time of love. Old-timers tend to want to douse the new couple with buckets of warnings—as if in doing so, it will ease the pain of coming trials.

I don't know why old, married folk are so prone to do this; they're just wasting their breath. When young lovers are in Eden, *they can't hear or see anyone but each other anyway.* So we may as well rejoice in their fresh love and join in the celebration of a new beginning. Don't hurry them too fast out of Eden. Let them stay and savor this very special time for as long as it lasts. The memory of the beautiful honeymoon in Eden may be exactly what sustains them through the more difficult gardens to come.

It would be the memory of Eden and the fellowship between God and humans once relished there that would sustain Jesus through His sacrifice to come.

You were the seal of perfection,
Full of wisdom and perfect in beauty.
You were in Eden, the garden of God.
(Ezek. 28:12b–13a, NKJV)

chapter twenty
ACHING IN GETHSEMANE

There is another garden, a garden of suffering, disillusionment, and pain. Why even look at it here in this book about relaxing and enjoying life? Because some of you reading this book today are walking through this particular garden. And though there is sorrow and excruciating pain there, there's comfort available, and a huge part of being able to relax and enjoy life has to do with finding peace in our gardens of deepest pain.

So come into this garden, the Garden of Gethsemane, and together we'll find a place of solace and refuge.

Gethsemane was an olive garden east of Jerusalem, a quiet place where Jesus had come before. That night, He came seeking comfort. His human and godly emotions were splitting open and ready to burst. The Gospel writers said "he began to be sorrowful and troubled," "he was in anguish." Jesus, Himself, said, "My soul is overwhelmed with sorrow to the point of death." He felt every painful emotion we feel, and then some. We will never know the depth of the pain the Father and Son suffered on our behalf that night. We do know that when Jesus needed His human friends the most—in those lonely, cold, early hours of morning—they were asleep and unavailable.

I've not been through much real suffering in my life. But I've known my own sorrows and pains, and I have many close friends with whom I've walked through deep valleys. I know it is hardest to bear a loss or fear of the future in the wee hours of the morning—when the world is dark and your friends are all sleeping peacefully, blissfully unaware of your tears.

None of us gets out of this world without some portion of pain. Death. Broken vows. Bankruptcy. Betrayal. Illness. These times are frightening, making us feel as though all that we depended on, all that was once solid and unshakable, is taken out from under us. Questions come pouring, one on top of another. "What's the purpose for this? Where's the reason? My God, have You forsaken me?"

If it weren't for this Garden of Gethsemane and the fact that Jesus so obviously felt the wrenching of sorrow and despair, and even asked similar questions of His own to the Father, I might be angry at God. But Jesus knows this place of suffering and questions; that's why He's supremely qualified to comfort us in our darkest nights.

There are major sorrows, but like big Eden moments, these don't happen that often in our human experience. More often come plain ol' really bad days. I'm remembering one in particular.

The morning began with a call from Scott. He'd just backed into a parked car on his way to work. He was fine, but the other car was not. Wondering how much that might set us back, I walked to the mailbox and there waiting for me was a most unkind letter. The sort that makes you feel as though you were just punched in the stomach—unaware and unprepared.

Reeling from that, I walked into the house wiping at my tears as I reread the letter, trying to comprehend why someone would write this. Just then I heard rain begin to fall, then a tremendous CLAP! as our house was struck by lightning. (Yes, this was one of those strikes that knocked out the computer's modem and the television set.) The total damage came to about $700. The deductible on our insurance was—you guessed it—$700.

That afternoon some old friends of ours called and asked us to meet them for dinner at a restaurant forty miles away. I thought it might be a much needed diversion. We waited in the restaurant for two hours for our friends who never showed up. Turns out they'd been waylaid by an approaching tornado.

On our drive home, with thunderclouds looming and rain pelting at our car's windshield, one of our headlights went out. We were spotted in our vehicle's one-eyed condition by an eager and alert highway patrolman—the sort who delights in writing tickets to miserable families on dark and gloomy nights.

After the patrolman gave Scott the ominous piece of paper, we morosely watched him walk back to the patrol car and drive off. At this point I began to sing pitifully, "The sun will come out—tomorrow. . . ."

I crooned too quickly.

The next day as I was preparing the kids an after-school snack, the radio announced that a tornado was heading in our direction. The worst part of this news for me was that I would have to figure out a way to clear a big enough space in our overstuffed closet to hold me and four children. Somehow I managed to pack us all in. Once the winds died down, and we were sure we had missed the tornado's path, I pried the kids out of the closet and told them what we needed was a fun trip to Wal-Mart.

Don't ask me why, but there's nothing like a trip to Wal-Mart to cheer me and the kids right up. Ours is one of those super-stores—bright and cheery, with room to spread out and breathe. Something for everyone to look at and whine for. In no time, we were there.

As the kids and I were loading up the basket, we suddenly realized that everyone else was moving quickly toward the front of the store. Thinking it was a blue light special and not one to miss a good bargain, I followed the crowd at a good clip, pushing my cart and hanging on to the children at the same time. Then I noticed the cashiers and salespeople were exiting the store too. When I asked one of them what was going on, they yelled, "Everyone out of the store—there's been a bomb threat!"

Outside in the parking lot with my kids and a cart full of unbought groceries (that I could not take home or bring back in the store to pay for) I began to pray. It was not a pretty prayer. *OK, Lord, I've had it!* I inwardly yelled. *Where would You like me to go to unwind from yesterday's stress—that isn't in the path of a tornado or being targeted for bombing, that is?*

During times like these I just want to say, "Wait, wait, wait—*whoa!* I just need to catch my breath a minute before the next disaster strikes." These things do have a way of coming in bunches, don't they? There must be a reason for such "seasons" of testing. (The bomb threat, thankfully, was a fake.)

One thing I know: There's comfort available for both major trials and life's unending series of little pains. It's the same comfort that was given to Christ in His deepest hour of need. Let's go back to the Garden of Gethsemane.

There are two things in the garden that both comforted Jesus and strengthened Him for His coming ordeal. First of all, *He had to come to a place of acceptance.*

It wasn't easy—not even for the Son of God. "If it is possible, may this cup be taken from me. Yet not, as I will, but as You will." There is a certain peace that comes from having struggled with all the possible solutions and finally accepting God's will.

Second, there is another comforting truth: *The ultimate purpose of suffering is joy.* We're told that angels came to minister to Christ in this garden. I don't know all they did, but I believe they pointed Christ toward the joy to come after the suffering was over—the joy awaiting in the next garden. Hebrews 12:2 tells us that Jesus, for "the joy set before Him endured the cross."

"Suffering prepares us for and increases our capacity for joy," says Vine's Concordance. That's a quote worth pondering. Is it really true? Will our suffering make joys to come that much sweeter? Yes, I believe it is true.

Often, perhaps more often than we realize, we get to see some of the joy that results from a time of suffering while we're here on this earth. But sometimes, there's no explanation forthcoming for pain suffered here; we simply have to hold on and believe that our day of joy is coming. I believe that those who've suffered the most on earth will have the greatest experience of joy when they burst into heaven: paraplegics soaring over heaven with new bodies, beloved husbands and wives and children shouting with joy at their reunion, all of us laughing with Jesus as we realize everything we suffered on earth was nothing compared to this—this joy beyond imagination.

A word of caution: When people have just been "hit" with something painful—when they've just recently stumbled into this garden—it's probably not the best time to offer these thoughts. Say nothing; just be there—a loving shoulder for them to cry on, a quiet presence without pressure. They need their time in this garden of sorrow, time to cry their tears and not be pushed forward toward the next phase too soon.

But there will come a time when life begins again. And this is the time when you can gently help point your hurting friends toward the next garden.

For we do not have a High Priest who cannot sympathize with our weaknesses. . . . Let us therefore come boldly to the throne of grace, that we may obtain mercy and find grace to help in time of need.
(Heb. 4:15–16, NKJV)

chapter twenty-one
RESURRECTING THE JOY!

After the dark night of Gethsemane, Eden's joy comes again. Only this time, it's deeper, stronger, even more precious. It is a joy that's been tested by fire. For the saying is profoundly true: *Suffering increases our capacity for joy.*

Come with me now into the wondrous third garden.

This garden belonged to a man named Joseph of Arimathea. He donated it to be used as a sheltering tomb for the tortured, lifeless body of Christ.

It became, instead, a launching pad.

For this is the brightest and best of all gardens: the Garden of the Resurrection, the garden place of renewal, rejoicing—"joy found again." Shades of Eden are now revisited. But this new Easter joy is even greater than Eden's original joy.

When Jesus appeared at the tomb, it took my breath away when I read that Mary did not recognize Him at first. She recognized the angels—after all, they were dressed in lightning white. But Jesus chose to appear to Mary apparently looking very much like a *gardener.* And that's who she thought He was—at first.

Back in Eden, the original Gardener appeared in the cool of the day. On one fateful occasion, however, the Gardener called out for His children, but Adam and Eve, having sinned, ran and hid. In this Garden of Resurrection, this Gardener/Savior was found walking again in the cool of the day. Again He called out a name—"Mary." This time, rather than running away, the child in the garden ran *toward* Him, crying, "Rabboni! Teacher!" What glorious contrast in scenes.

I think of the resurrection gardens in my own life—times when I experienced a second, more profound joy for having gone through a Gethsemane experience.

Marriage comes to mind. Scott and I started out blissfully in Eden. We thought no one had ever loved or would ever love each other as much we did. It was perfect.

Then little things began to eat at that perfect picture we had of each other, and one morning, we woke up thinking, "Hmmm . . . don't believe we're in Eden anymore."

We, like many couples, hit our Gethsemane. This is where most people throw in the towel and say, "I'll pass on this cup, thank you very much." We fussed and fought and agonized, but eventually came to accept that this marriage, our cup, was God's will for our lives.

Then eventually came the resurrection of love and joy. And oh, how much deeper and real our love is for each other now, having survived the trials. Much more precious even than our Eden honeymoon joy.

Most of us walk through the three gardens in our relationship with God. As young children we have a free and easy trusting relationship with God. We're in Eden. Then disillusionment, religious standards, fear, and failure come into our lives, and we wonder if God's all we once hoped and thought He was.

If we make it through this phase, we often find ourselves giving up on trying to please God, which is exactly where He wants us. We come back to Him as an adult for having been through the pain, but we also come to Him more a child than ever, deeply aware of our need for His love and help. And that's where the real joy lies after a time of pain and confusion—resting in the arms of Father.

As the snake confused Eve in the garden, he still slinks about trying to confuse us today. Paul warned, "I'm afraid that exactly as the Snake seduced Eve with his smooth patter, you are being lured away from the simple purity of your love for Christ." In other words, don't let a lying snake take away your joy of simply walking as a child with his Father in the garden of life.

Whatever garden we find ourselves in from day to day or moment to moment—whether it leans more toward Eden or Gethsemane or toward a garden of renewal and resurrection—it is a comfort to know there is a Gardener waiting to weep with us or rejoice with us according to our need. He is our Jubilee, our source of refreshment, in every garden of life.

Contemplating these things on my drive home from church, I wrote another little ditty on the back of a napkin.

The Gardener

I walked with my God in the cool of the day
In the beginning when Eden was new

A View from the Porch Swing

And we laughed as we walked in that beautiful world
Full of hopes and dreams to come true

In each Garden I'm in, The Gardener's my friend
He's walked these paths before me
He's there in the sunshine
He's there in the rain
And He knows just what my soul needs

I stumbled into a garden of pain
Blinded by tears and my grief
But there in the darkness He held out His hand
Promising never to leave

In each Garden I'm in, The Gardener's my friend
He's walked these paths before me
He's there in the sunshine
He's there in the rain
And He knows just what my soul needs

I walked toward a tomb in the cool of the day
Alone now, with nothing the same
But wait—there's The Gardener
My Savior
My Friend
He's risen and calling my name

In each Garden I'm in, The Gardener's my friend
He's walked these paths before me
He's there in the sunshine
He's there in the rain
and He knows just what my soul needs

RESURRECTING THE JOY!

He will comfort all her waste places;
He will make her wilderness like Eden,
And her desert like the garden of the LORD;
Joy and gladness will be found in it,
Thanksgiving and the voice of melody.
(Isa. 51:3, NKJV)

chapter twenty-two
OVERCOMING WITH WORMS

(I know we've been diving into some of my deep thoughts, but I should warn you—we're about to head upstream into more shallow headwaters.)

Many authors these days have a symbol of their own unique personality. When we think of Barbara Johnson, we visualize geraniums in broad-rimmed hats. When picturing Chuck Swindoll, a Harley Davidson roars to mind. When *Worms in My Tea* appeared in bookstores, I never dreamed my name would be forever intertwined with a slimy invertebrate.

To make matters worse, in the publishing world, a book's title is most often given a shortened nickname to simplify communication. While touring my publishing company for the first time, an eager young woman introduced me to a group of salespeople by proudly announcing, "This is Becky Freeman—she's our author with *Worms.*" (Don't you know how eager they were to shake hands with me after that intro?) Since that happening, I've played around with the idea of changing my business card to read:

Becky Freeman
"The Author with *Worms.*"

Or better yet, I've thought about using the name *Worms* as an acronym for my own organization. But what would I want the acronym to stand for? (Not to mention who or what could *I* possibly organize?) This morning I found myself shouting, "I've got it!" as I was struck with inspiration. May I present the name of my proposed organization:

WORMS, INC.
Women **O**vercoming **R**idiculous, **M**ind-boggling **S**ituations ©.

This says it all; because I've accepted my life's purpose and mission, which is to encourage like-minded women who are struggling to overcome the ridiculous and mind-boggling situations life throws our way, through my writing and speaking and driving into muddy ditches. I looked up the word *ridiculous* in my thesaurus this morning. It means "absurd, ludicrous, preposterous, asinine, nonsensical, foolish, silly, idiotic, irrational, unreasonable, senseless, outlandish, laughable, comical, funny, droll, amusing, farcical, crazy." When I showed this to Scott, he asked, "Are you sure you're not looking up the word *Becky?*"

"No," I answered indignantly, "my name is closer to *mind-boggling,* which means 'extraordinary, phenomenal, remarkable, amazing, incredible, astounding, indescribable' and, my personal favorite, 'stunning.' "

"Yep, you're a little Stun Gun, Hon."

The first lesson a WORM must learn is to take comments like my husband's at face value. So I simply said, "Thank you." To which he replied, "No comment."

To assume the leadership of such a prestigious organization as WORMS, INC., one must, of course, have the necessary qualifications and experience. Besides the volumes I've already written, I'd like to submit the following story of how I persevered in overcoming a recent series of ridiculous, mind-boggling circumstances. It should demonstrate why I'm most qualified to pilot WORMS.

This past Thanksgiving our family was visiting Scott's parents, who live about two hours driving distance from us. Scott and the children decided to stay over for an extra day, but I needed to get back home to work on a writing assignment. Since we had driven two cars, I drove home alone, leaving late that evening so I could get an early start the next morning. On the drive home, I went the wrong direction several times because it was dark and, well, you know how different the world looks when the lights are off. But I overcame this adversity by driving through several all-night fast-food places until finally happening upon a teenager with sufficient wits to point me in the right direction.

When I arrived at the gate to the entrance of our little lakeside community, it was around 2:00 A.M., and I found myself in the first of a series of mind-boggling predicaments. I hadn't remembered to get a key to the gate from Scott. I contemplated turning away and driving to a motel, but thought, *No, that would be silly. Our house is only a mile down the road there beyond this locked gate. Surely I can figure out a way to get around the gate and to the house.* Then I remembered a roundabout, backroads entrance the kids had once shown me. All I'd have to do is drive through a pasture, around some ponds and trees, and over and up a couple of hills.

I turned the wheels of my little Subaru and headed toward the pasture. I got maybe a hundred yards before I realized I was driving in grass-camouflaged mud. With the sun long since gone to bed, I could not tell whether the dark thing looming in front of me was a hill, a pond, or a tree. I realized neither of the three would be particularly good news. So praying hard, I backed out carefully—slipping and sliding, but never getting stuck—and landed right back at my starting place in front of the massive locked gate. At least my Subaru and I were not wound around a tree or at the bottom of a fish pond, but still there was the gate to contend with.

More determined than ever to get home alone, I parked on the side of the road, took my keys and my purse, locked the doors to my car, and walked up to the seven-foot gate. Tossing my purse over the top, I waited until I heard it land with a thud on the other side, then I began my ascent over the gate. A middle-aged woman doesn't get many chances to climb fences, and I actually thought it was rather fun. Like being in the third grade again. Of course, I'd rather have enjoyed this jaunty climb on a sunny day, rather than on a cold, misty night at 2:00 A.M.—but we overcomers must look on the bright side, mustn't we?

I picked up my purse from the asphalt, resolutely slinging it over my shoulder, and began the mile-long trek to our home. Have I mentioned how dark it was yet? Living in the country, there are no illuminating boosts from nearby city lights. I felt like Snow White walking through cartoon shadowy forests, the trees taking on a dark life of their own on either side of the road. The hoot owls once made me jump with a such a start that I dropped my purse and had to grope for it on the ground like a blind woman.

I kept repeating comforting verses I'd learned as a child: "At times I am afraid I will trust in Thee," "You are a very present help in times of trouble." Before long my heart stopped pounding, and I was actually beginning to enjoy the quiet night and the stars overhead. Until my new boots rubbed two fresh blisters into the sides of my tender feet. I was also beginning to feel the painful effects of having downed a supersized cola on the drive home.

Finally, thankfully, I made my way to my front door and nearly fell on the welcoming front porch with gratitude. "Ah, home sweet home," I said, leaning against the door to open it. But something was awry with my home sweet home. The door was locked. Now, I realize that for most people this is not unusual. Most folk lock the front doors of their houses when they go away for any length of time. But since we were only gone for the day and Scott knew I'd be coming home alone, a locked door raised all sorts of dire suspicions. Then I realized something else: The dogs weren't barking. Daisy, our Brittany spaniel, and Colonel, the little schnauzer, *always* bark either in greeting to us or in warning to strangers. Something was terribly wrong with this picture, besides the fact that the door was locked, and I was once again, keyless (not to mention, clueless).

Burglars, obviously, had killed the dogs and locked me out of my own house. I hate it when that happens. But "we shall overcome" is my motto, so I did not give up. I would go find help.

However, where does one go for help, on foot, at 3:35 A.M.? My feet bleeding, my head pounding, I grabbed up my purse and marched toward our neighbors, Melissa and Michael Gantt. *Yes!* I brightened when I saw their car in the driveway, *At least they are in town.* I hated to wake them up at this hour, but I felt, for my own safety, that I had to get someone to help me find a way into my house and who'd provide comfort if I should need to grieve the loss of my pets and all worldly possessions.

I knocked and knocked. And knocked and knocked. Not a creature would stir in my neighbor's house. I turned the knob, and to my surprise the front door popped open. "Melissa!" I yelled. Nothing. "Michael!" I hollered. Still all was quiet. *Great,* I thought, *maybe the burglar got Michael and Melissa too.* So I walked into the darkened kitchen, noticed a phone with glowing buttons, picked it up, and dialed Scott's parents' home.

"Beverly?"

"Yes?"

"I'm so sorry for calling this late. Or this early. I guess it's morning, isn't it? Can I please speak to Scott? I've broken into my neighbor's house, and I'm using their phone because I can't break into our house."

"What?"

"It's a long story. Could I just speak with Scott?"

"Sure," she answered, and in a few seconds, Scott was on the phone.

"Becky?" he asked sleepily.

"Yes?"

"Why am I talking to you on the phone at 4:00 in the morning?"

"Well, Scott . . ." and I explained what had happened up to that point. "So you see," I continued, "I'm worried because the doors are locked and the dogs are probably dead. And I'm in someone else's house without their knowledge, using their phone to talk to you. And they may be dead, too, but I'm too afraid to go look and see."

"Don't you dare, Becky," Scott said quickly. "You are lucky Michael hasn't woken up and shot you, thinking you are an intruder."

"I *am* an intruder, just a friendly one."

"But they don't know that!"

"What should I do?" I lowered my voice to a whisper.

"Go home. I locked the doors this morning and forgot to tell you. The dogs are probably over at George's house down the street. You know how they love to go over there when we're gone—he's always feeding them treats and letting them in for a visit."

"How will I get in?"

"Climb through the side window."

"Gotcha. See ya tomorrow—if I'm alive and all."

"You'll be fine."

I gently put the phone down, wondered if I should risk using the Gantt's restroom before I left, decided my bladder would have to tough it out, and tiptoed back out of the front door, forcing my aching feet back to my home. I had to get a ladder to reach the unlocked window, but once inside, I nearly kissed the linoleum. The dogs were nowhere to be seen, and the house was completely ransacked—exactly as we had left it. I breathed a sigh of relief, ran to the bathroom to take care of my most pressing need, then took a hot bath, put Band-Aids on my blisters, and fell into bed. Scott called just to make sure I hadn't killed myself climbing through the window. I assured him I was fine and that if there were burglars hiding in the house, I no longer cared—as long as they went about their work quietly and let me sleep. *All is well,* I thought as I finally fell into a deep slumber. *Only you, Lord, make me dwell in safety. Thank you for taking care of me. Together, we have overcome.*

I'd been asleep a full hour before the phone rang. I checked the red digital numbers on the alarm clock: 5:30 A.M. Picking up the phone, I wearily answered, "Hello?"

"Becky?" the voice on the other end sounded concerned.

"Yes?"

"This is Janet—I live near the gate."

"Yes, Janet, what's up?"

"Well, I'm sorry to call so early but the paperboy came by this morning and gave me a credit card belonging to you. Said he found it on the ground near the gate."

I explained what had transpired the night before, and Janet offered to pick me up, take me to the gate, and open it with her key. I accepted her offer—this way I could also get my car off the road and check for any more credit cards that might have fallen out of my purse when I threw it over the gate. When I got to the gate—sure enough—I found another credit card sticking out of a pile of leaves. I thanked Janet for her help and told her to pass on my gratitude to the paperboy, then drove back home.

You know, I'd better check my purse to see if there are any more cards missing, I thought before I dropped back in bed. But now, my purse was nowhere to be found. I looked everywhere I could have possibly left it. "I can't believe this!" I yelled aloud to an empty house. Then I realized what probably happened. *I must have left my purse outside the window when I crawled in the house. A burglar must have seen it there in the porch light and stolen it!*

I dialed the sheriff's office. It was now 6:15 A.M., and I'd had more activity all night long than I get in most days. When the dispatcher picked up the phone, I said, "Yes, this is Becky Freeman. I just wanted to report a stolen purse, in case you recover any of my checks or credit cards or anything."

"And where was your purse stolen?"

"It was stolen where I left it outside last night when I crawled through the window to get into my house." I explained as best I could what had transpired during the night and my theory on my purse's disappearance. The dispatcher seemed anxious to get off the phone but wished me the best in locating the purse snatcher.

I'd better call the Village Market, too, I thought, *just in case someone tries to cash one of my checks there. It's the closest place for a burglar to try to pull something like that.* Michael and Melissa are not only our neighbors and friends, they also own the Village Market. Melissa answered the phone.

"Hello, Gantt's Village Market, can I help you?"

"Melissa?"

"Becky?"

"Melissa! You're not dead!"

"No," she sounded confused, "but I feel like it. I had to open the store this morning, and Michael and I had both taken antihistamines last night for our colds. I'm still having a hard time keeping my eyes open. Becky?"

"Yes?"

"The weirdest thing happened—we found your purse in our kitchen this morning."

I was so embarrassed. After I explained my breaking and entering to Melissa, I called back the sheriff's department.

"Please don't worry any more about my missing purse," I explained jubilantly. "I found it! I left it in the other house I broke into last night! Isn't that wonderful?"

The dispatcher agreed that it was and quickly hung up the phone.

Relieved to have located my purse, and exhausted, I fell back into bed and into a deep sleep—for an entire thirty minutes—before the phone rang again at 7:00 A.M. Still a mite early to be getting calls on a weekend morning. I picked up the phone and recognized the sweet voice of another friend and neighbor, Wally. (Out in the country, most neighbors are friendly.)

"Becky?" There was something oddly familiar about the way this conversation was starting.

"Yes?"

"Becky, I was jogging this morning and about halfway between the gate and your house, I found three of your credit cards!"

"Oh, Wally, thank you! I must have dropped them out of my purse when that owl hooted." Then I went through the entire story again with Wally, who sounded even more confused by the time I'd finished. I had to admit, the saga was getting more complicated with every phone call. The next day, my son found the last missing credit card on the road while riding his bike. Apparently, I'd been like Gretel of fairy-tale fame in those wee morning hours, only instead of dropping crumbs I'd been dropping credit cards to mark my path.

I am so blessed to have friends and neighbors who are honest and caring, the kind who understand when you get locked out of the gate and have to climb over it and walk home at three o'clock in the morning. And when you can't get in, they understand when you break into their house and leave your purse but you don't know it so you have to call the sheriff and report it stolen, and then, when you find out it wasn't, have to call back and retract the report. They understand when you have to crawl through the window of your own house because you have no keys to anything whatsoever and that you leave credit cards strewn over a mile-long length of road. Well, maybe they don't understand. But they do try to be supportive in my struggle to be a WORM: a woman overcoming yet another string of ridiculous, mind-boggling situations.

So, WORMS of the world, wriggle out to the porch and relax. Not only is there now a support group for us, but we can hold our heads up out of the dirt with pride as we realize anew our purpose on earth: to give the rest of the world a chance to pause, scratch their heads, and ask, *"What?"*

God provided a worm.
(Jonah 4:7)

chapter twenty-three
CALMING DOWN WITH PETS

It had been a long, hard summer without a shower and shave. The Colonel was beyond needing a homemade, garden-variety haircut; it was time for a professional barber. Or a *groomer,* as they call it in the doggy world.

So early one morning I dropped our miniature schnauzer off at Country Kennels Grooming Salon to see if they could salvage what was left of him. When I went back to pick him up, I could hardly believe the transformation. There on the grooming table stood a champion of a dog: his back shaved close, his silvery "skirt" combed out like silk, the irresistible dark eyes peering beneath bushy eyebrows, his snout adorned with the classic schnauzer mustache.

"I can't believe it!" I shouted, "Colonel looks fantastic!"

"Oh," said the lady, shaking her head, "that's not Colonel. Here's *your* dog."

She opened one of the cages to let a sad-looking animal come slinking out. As I gently lifted my pitiful pet to my arms, I couldn't help but comment. "He's naked."

"I'm sorry, Mrs. Freeman," the lady across the counter said kindly. "We did the best we could. His hair was so matted and tangled we basically had to shave everything off. We are dog groomers, not miracle workers."

I paid our bill, then Colonel and I hung our heads and walked out the door in shame. I vowed never to let a dog of mine go through such a humiliating experience again.

So now I scrounge up the money to have Colonel professionally groomed at least once every two months. And it is worth it. These days he's holding his furry schnauzer snout high; his silvery/black skirt is combed silken soft. Most evenings, Colonel sits in my lap as I stroke his fur and talk baby talk to him. In spite of myself, a mutt has wrapped himself around my heart. An animal has turned yet another human into a blabbering idiot. (Even at the doggy barber they refer to me as "Colonel's Mommy.")

Daisy, our eight-year-old, rust-and-white Brittany spaniel is also tugging at our heartstrings these days. We've never owned a pet long enough to see it age. They've always met with an untimely death, usually in the prime of their lives. (There was the unfortunate kitten that fell into the fan belt; various animals that have fallen beneath car wheels; Rachel's rat that committed suicide by jumping out of its cage into Colonel's mouth; and that one awful time I accidentally blew up Zeke's ferret by feeding it leftover Mexican casserole.)

But Daisy's been a true survivor of the Freeman Family Farm. So it astounds and saddens me to realize that almost overnight Daisy's gone from a young marathon rabbit-chaser to a dog-bed-bound old lady. Her hind legs shake with arthritis; her great joys are sleeping, eating, and getting her belly rubbed. Gone are the days when she challenged every passing car to a race. "Ah, let 'em win," she seems to say as she rests her head on her paws, lazily watching them pass. I don't know when it happened, but sometime this year Daisy bequeathed most car-chasing duties to her chipper subordinate, Colonel. However, Daisy's not so old that she'll let Colonel have her bed. Not that he hasn't tried.

Colonel's been coveting Daisy's large dog bed for months. Every time Daisy rises to get a drink of water or go outside to relieve herself, Colonel makes a mad dash for Daisy's king-size sleeping quarters. Feeling sorry for Colonel, I bought him his own bed. But no, this would not do. I came home one day to find Colonel sitting contentedly in Daisy's bed again. His bed? He ate it. Pieces of fabric and foam lay strewn all over the house.

"Colonel!" I scolded, "That's it. You are not getting another bed of your own. And guess what? You can't have Daisy's either! Now OUTSIDE!"

I'm telling you, living with these two is like having little kids again. (Except that one of them is old and arthritic.) But I cannot imagine our household without these dogs. I was ecstatic to see them when they came bounding up the morning after their disappearance when I thought the burglar had gotten them. (Apparently, since we had abandoned them for the day, they enjoyed an overnight Thanksgiving stay with another family in the neighborhood.) They've gone from "strictly outside animals" to lap-sitting babies. From pets to parts of our family. I've never considered myself more than an "animal liker," but in my old age, I have to admit I've been won over. I'm fast on my way to becoming an animal lover. Thankfully, I hear this is good for my health.

According to medical studies, "among people who suffer a heart attack, pet owners have one-fifth the death rate of the pet-less." (Of course the studies don't say what caused the heart attacks in the first place. I'd wager that a few of the pet owners' attacks happened when they discovered Fifi's unwelcome pet deposit on their new lace bedspread.) The benefits appear to come not from increased exercise (you don't walk a pet lizard or fish), but in communicating with animals, stroking them, or just gazing at fish swimming in their tank.

Pets also make us healthy in other ways. First, they give recovering patients a living, breathing entity to get well for—because animals need their owners. Second, having a pet provides moments of pleasure and solace in hard times, and a pet's compelling needs can interrupt our bad times. When the dog has to go out, out goes an ongoing argument too. (I wonder if marriage counselors know this. They could train divorce-busting dogs—like they do seeing-eye dogs—that would automatically bark every time a couple had a twinge of irritation rise in their voices.) Third, pets give us unconditional acceptance. They love us in spite of the fact that we let their hair get wet and matted. (And we also love them in spite of the fact that they chew up their new dog beds.)

Animals also make fascinating study. I enjoyed listening to a tape series on "The Secret Life of Dogs." Granted, much of this author's musings are highly speculative—it's a virtual canine soap opera. Still, her intensive study of dogs and their habits made me much more aware of how intelligent and curious animals can be.

Gary Spence, country lawyer and author of *How to Argue and Win Every Time,* said he's learned more from his dog than from most people. For example, when Gary's dog wants some affection, he asks for it—he just puts his head in the author's lap and gazes into his eyes until he gets some strokes. I need to remember to try this with Scott the next time my affection-tank is running low.

If you don't own a pet because you think they would add stress to your life, you might want to reconsider. According to a March 1996 Associated Press article coming out of Buffalo, New York: "When it comes to times of stress, researchers find, the most reassuring companion isn't your sweetheart—it's your schnauzer. A new study found that people who were put into stressful situations showed the least amount of tension when accompanied by their dog. The stress levels were highest when the subjects were with their spouses." I wouldn't suggest getting rid of your spouse and replacing him or her with a dog. But for your health and well-being you just might discover that caring for an animal, and having it care for you, could turn out to be one of life's unexpected jubilees.

Who provides food for the raven
When its young ones cry to God? . . .
Do you know the time when the mountain goats bear young?
Or can you mark when the deer gives birth? . . .
Who set the wild donkey free? . . .
Have you given the horse strength? . . .
Does the hawk fly by your wisdom?
(Questions from God, the ultimate "pet owner," when He spoke out of the whirlwind to Job.)
(Job 38:41; 39:1, 5, 19, 26, NKJV)

chapter twenty-four

PARING DOWN LIFE

Unless your life's been too complex to notice, you've probably observed that one of the major new trends in "Boomerville" today is what's being labeled as *voluntary simplicity*. (Much of it is really *involuntary* simplicity, but our generation has its pride. We don't like to think of ourselves as being *forced* to simplify our lives because, say, our company's downsized and we've been laid off. Or that we went bankrupt from playing fast and loose with credit cards. We Baby Boomers prefer to see this as a *voluntary* thing.)

One small, tan book, *Simplify Your Life,* is near the forefront of this new wave of cutting back, slowing up, paring down, opting out, and moving away—to John Wayne-sounding places like Montana and Wyoming and the Texas hill country. In an interview with the *New York Times,* the author of the book, Elaine St. James, is quoted as saying, "I was sitting at my desk one day, and my schedule was full of phone calls and appointments and meetings with people, and I realized this was just not what I wanted to do." She continued, "I had finally reached a point I think many of us reach—of despair. We're tired of these complex lives and never having time to ourselves. I think the despair is coming from our souls."

According to the article, Ms. St. James gave up her job in real estate, threw away masses of extra stuff, moved from a 3,000-square-foot home to a 600-square-foot condominium. She even pared down her wardrobe to three basic colors: black, gray, and white. And get this ladies: "She reduced her purse to a rubber band around a credit card, library card, license, and money."

I mentioned these facts to my friend Gracie over lunch recently.

"Well," Gracie commented, her fork punctuating the air, "I've about had it with all this talk of simplicity. It makes me feel way too guilty about wanting an interesting, busy life—with reds and purples in my wardrobe. I think I'll write a book called *Complicate Your Life.*"

I have to admit, I could add plenty of personal material to Gracie's book concept. However, I do have a few simplifying tips of my own I could probably submit to Ms. St. James. Since she already has her own book, though, I think I'll just keep my ideas and share them with you. May I present "Becky's Hints for the Simpleminded":

1. On Matching Socks

In a word, don't. I'm telling you, trying to pair socks is a dead-end job. I know the Nike commercial says, "Just do it." But they are talking about shoes. They need a commercial for socks, that says, "Don't bother." Sure, a tennis shoe is known to sneak off now and then (is that why they call them "sneakers"?), but generally it turns up after a few minutes of its owner's pawing under the couch.

Socks, on the other hand (or in this case, on the other *foot*) can't be trusted to stay faithful to one another even if you staple them, tie them in a knot, and have them repeat vows. I have no idea where their mates run off to or why they do it so quickly and permanently. (In desperation Erma Bombeck once told her children that missing socks "go to live with Jesus." I wonder if her kids pictured angels flying around heaven wearing a colorful array of mismatched socks.) Since it seems that socks are intent on staying single, my advice is, "Quit fighting them."

Our family has simplified our life by having one giant laundry basket (The Sock Single's Joint) where I dump all socks as they come out of the dryer. I mean *everyone's* socks: from Scott's dress socks to Rachel's scrunchy socks to Gabe's crusty, holey ones. In the morning, it is every sibling and spouse for himself (or *herself*, as the case may be). I usually just close my eyes and reach in the basket (as if it's a grab bag) and slip my cold feet into whatever I happen to pull up. Of course, I work at home where no one cares that I'm wearing an orange scrunch sock on one foot and a man's navy dress sock on the other.

2. Being on Time

In contrast to most time managers' advice, I have my own simple theory about helping turn the chronically late into the consistently punctual: Forget it.

If you are a chronically late person, more than likely you will always be a chronically late person. (Isn't that what *chronic* means—ongoing, never ceasing?) Life will be simpler when you and everyone else accept this.

Here's what I suggest to my tardy-hardy comrades: Only make friends with other time-impaired people. Screen all future acquaintances. Choose from people that you spy running from parking lots to meeting places while they're simultaneously applying lipstick and straightening their panty hose. You can be sure they will sympathize with your belated behaviors. However, if you just can't keep yourself from forming a relationship with some interesting, albeit punctual, person, do yourself a favor and give them the straight scoop right from the start. Here's what I say in my debriefing speech to organized, on-schedule friends:

> Look. You should know this up front: I'm a late person. When people introduce me as The Late Becky Freeman, I'm not dead, I am just running behind. It's what I do—run behind. (I see this as my own generous way of allowing others to go *ahead*.)
>
> I'm friendly, I'm loyal, I can even be fairly entertaining—once I arrive at my destination, which will be, by the way, at least twenty minutes late. I'm not saying this habit of mine is justifiable. It is not, and I hope someday I'll experience the thrill of knowing what it is like to arrive on time for a lunch date without having to sprint from the car to the restaurant table. But until then, you'll save yourself a lot of grief if you'll just tell me to meet you twenty to thirty minutes earlier than you actually plan to show up. Or you could bring along a good book to read or some correspondence to catch up on so you'll be relaxed right up until the moment when I burst through the door, breathlessly apologizing for being late. Think it over carefully. Are you *sure* you still want to be friends?

A "late" friend of mine explains herself by wearing a button that says simply, "This is the earliest I've ever been late."

3. Organizing Silverware

I know this advice of mine may sound repetitive, but again my advice boils down to this: Simply don't do it. Throw out time-consuming little sorting trays and just dump the knives, forks, and spoons straight out of the dishwasher basket into an open drawer. In two seconds, the job's done. I actually owe this hint to my mother-in-law, Beverly. She's been dumping silverware haphazardly for years, and, so far, no one's stood at the drawer in a fit of confusion saying, "Will somebody help me? I simply can't tell a spoon from a fork if they aren't stacked together into neat, little compartments." If someone in your family can't pick out the utensil they need from the rest of the bunch, they have more problems than presorting their flatware would solve.

4. Cooking

My cousin Jamie wrote me a letter describing how she recently discovered a way to simplify the baking of goodies for her children.

She'd been buying packaged cookies for years, but eventually her children tasted the Real McCoy cookies: homemade treats from Grandma's house. From that moment, they began begging Jamie to make some real—from scratch—sugar cookies. Jamie gave being Betty Crocker a valiant try, but, alas, after the dough balls were placed in a hot oven, she discovered to her surprise that they melted and grew. When she opened the door to take a peek at her creation, the kids were distraught.

"We didn't want pancakes!" they cried. "We asked for cookies!"

Jamie consoled them, and the next day, she bought several beautiful cookies from the local bakery, spread them on a cookie sheet, and then—just a moment before the children came in the door from school—popped the whole thing in the oven to warm them. When she pulled the warm tray of confections out of the oven, the children never asked any questions and Jamie only felt a slight twinge of guilt when she heard them bragging and sharing "our mom's homemade cookies" with the neighborhood kids.

5. Mornings

To nonmorning people, my suggestion—if at all possible—is to begin early on training your family so that one day, you, too, may be able to avoid functioning in the early a.m. altogether.

It has taken me years to get to this luxurious stage of life, but I am no longer an active participant in mornings. The surprising thing is that I'm convinced my four children are better off and more responsible because of it. (Besides, I'm one less body to contend with in the family bathroom.)

Rachel, my most responsible child, rises early, takes a shower, and wakes up her brothers. (This child also irons and lays out her clothes every night before school. She even keeps a chart so that at a moment's notice she can tell you what she was wearing three weeks ago Tuesday.) Zach, my oldest son, makes the coffee and drives them all to school. Zeke, the closest thing to a gourmet cook in our family (*gourmet cook* being defined as "one who makes food without charring it"), puts some semblance of breakfast out on the counter. Gabe, the youngest, couldn't care less what he wears but spends a good deal of his morning gooping up and styling his thick, dark hair. Scott, a better morning-kind-of-guy, gets up and has a father/children chat with the kids, makes sure they have lunch money, and sends them out the door with a cheerful wave. Then, before he heads to work, he pours me a cup of coffee with just the right amount of cream and sugar and brings it to me in bed.

As I said, it has taken me several years to arrange such a deal. First, I had to find a job that allowed me to enjoy a slow, morning-recovery time. (Another plus for the writing life.) I had to agonize through the Driver's Ed. Phase to get Zachary qualified to take over the morning drive. Then I had to train all four children how to pour just the right amount of cold cereal into a bowl and cover it, just so, with milk. The hardest part was convincing Scott that bringing a woman coffee in bed would not turn her into a lazy, spoiled brat. I finally convinced him that this little extra kindness to me in the morning would yield numerous rewards for the rest of the family in the late afternoon and evening. When they feel like zombies, I still have energy to clean up the kitchen and help with homework. It's a great system all around.

There is one drawback, however, in allowing a man to preside over the children in the morning. Most men have zero fashion sense. There is no telling what your children will wear out the door if your husband is in charge. I went up to the high school, not long ago, to drop off a paper for Zeke. The principal, Mr. White, called Zeke to the office for me, and when I saw him my mouth dropped open. I kid you not: There stood my fifteen-year-old son dressed in thermal underwear from his neck to his feet. He was wearing a pair of plaid shorts over the thermals, a pair of mountain climbing boots, and topped off the ensemble with a fuzzy, red, Santa Claus hat. I stared at Zeke then looked helplessly back at Mr. White.

The principal just shook his head and grinned. "Mrs. Freeman, I want you and your husband to know—whenever we see Zeke we think of your family."

6. Birthday Gifts

I don't know if other people's children make a habit of this, but my children tend to put off telling me vital information until the very last minute. For example, last night around 5:30 P.M., as I was putting a pan of chicken into the oven, my youngest son burst through the back door shouting, "The PTO Spaghetti Supper and Meet the Teacher Night is tonight! It starts at 6:00!" That was a shock, but the most common last-minute fiascoes seem to resolve around birthday parties.

"Oh, Mom!" one of them will yell, generally about the time I've climbed into the shower and soaked and lathered my hair. "I have to be at Joshua's birthday party in fifteen minutes!"

"Joshua has a birthday party *today?!?*" I'll yell back as I scurry to rinse the soap out. "Why didn't you tell me this sooner?"

"I forgot!" the panicky voice will shout through the door. "And we need to get him a present too!"

This scenario has repeated itself so often around our house that we've invented what we call "The Simplified Birthday Gift." Before we head out the door to the car, my hair still dripping wet, I'll instruct the kids to grab a ribbon and some crayons or markers. Then I drive to the nearest convenience store, ask the clerk for a brown paper bag, and working together as a team, we fill it up with assorted kid junk: bubblegum, Slow Pokes, gummy critters, Tootsie Rolls, taffy—if it will rot your teeth, it goes in the bag. After paying for the loot, we jump back in the car, where the kids decorate the bag with the crayons and tie it all up with the ribbon. And there you have it—a generic, all-purpose birthday gift, suitable for any child regardless of sex or age. Their parents may not be thrilled with it, but it's a surefire hit with the recipients.

I'm guessing that about half of the women—those of the creative, right-brained variety—who are reading this chapter will understand and applaud my hints for the simpleminded. The other half (the organized, logical ones) will worry about my sanity and the welfare of my children. That's understandable. Believe me, there are days when I, too, worry about my sanity and the welfare of my children. But then, every so often, something purely delightful happens that assures me I'm OK. Such a thing occurred this week.

Zeke called me from school to ask if I would mind letting him stay late to play tennis. "That's fine," I said. There was more to the request than Zeke had first indicated. "And, Mom," Zeke asked sweetly, "when you come to pick me up, would you mind taking four other kids home?" I breathed a heavy sigh. Out here in the country, kids don't live next door to each other; they live acres, miles, *whole counties* apart. But I'd not had much time with Zeke lately and rather missed his company, so I answered, "OK, Zeke. I'll take everyone home. I can't do it every day, but tell your friends I'll do delivery duty today."

"Thanks, Mom," Zeke said brightly. "We *really* appreciate it."

Later that afternoon, my compact car was stuffed to the hood with the sweaty bodies of five, lanky teenagers. Still, there's something about the exuberance of teens that I like, even when they smell really bad. We laughed at our sardine-packed cargo, and the kids teased me good-naturedly about my not-so-great driving. (I missed a couple of turns and ran over a few curbs—the usual.) After I'd delivered two of the kids, one boy in the back said, "Man, everybody at school likes you."

"Everybody likes who?" I asked, thinking he was talking to Zeke or one of the other kids.

"You, Mrs. Freeman. Everybody says, 'Man, Zeke's mom is so much fun.' "

"Really? They do?" I asked in genuine surprise.

"Oh, yeah. You, like, laugh a lot. My dad's got a good sense of humor, but he just doesn't use it much."

"Well, I'm really touched," I said sincerely. "You know I'm not much of a homemaking-type Mom, and sometimes I worry about that."

"Oh, man," the boy continued genuinely, "my mom cooks good meals, and she's a perfect housecleaner, but she hardly ever smiles. Everything's so serious. I think she'd rather have the house perfectly clean than sit down and talk and laugh with us kids. I'd rather have a messy house any day, as long as we could have more fun."

"Yeah," Zeke chimed in, a hint of pride in his voice. "I can say for a fact that Mom's never been boring. And she does keep us laughing."

Mark Twain once said he could live a good two months on one compliment. That car ride gave me enough encouragement to live on for four months. It also made me realize that when we talk about simplifying our lives, it doesn't necessarily mean that we won't sometimes land in wild, complicated, hectic situations (like agreeing to chauffeur five teenagers home in a small car).

To me, voluntary simplicity means intentionally keeping first things first: remembering to enjoy one another's company, to share God's love, and to laugh as often as possible. It's not so much about making the ride easier (although that has its benefits); it's more about choosing to find joy in this wild, wacky journey.

"But seek first the kingdom of God and His righteousness, and all these things shall be added to you."
(Matt. 6:33, NKJV)

chapter twenty-five

WEIGHING FOOD
IN BALANCE

Food, glorious food!

So when did it become so risky to eat it?

Am I the only one bewildered with counting calories, fat grams, sugar, and bran flecks? Just as soon as I got all the calorie counts memorized—of everything from a jelly doughnut (with and without glaze) to a quarter-inch sliced pickle—calories fell from nutritional grace. Now we have to find room in our overcrowded brains to store grams of fat.

By now you may have noticed that scientists love playing a game with the general population called "This Stuff Will Kill You." They come out with a new report showcasing the latest food that is destined to make us all keel over dead—if we don't stop consuming it, and *now*.

A few months later—just to keep us alert and alarmed—the illustrious experts change the game plan.

"Come to think of it," a newsbreaking article will report, "maybe we were a bit hasty last year. Turns out that the food we warned you about doesn't actually *kill* you. Is that what you thought we were saying? No, no, no. Actually, our latest research shows that eating this particular item, in fact, may help you live to be well over 120. Sorry about the mix-up. But stay tuned, one and all, for our next round of 'This Stuff Will Kill You.' " By the time we've all suffered through months of withdrawal from trying to disassociate our bodies from the so-called "deadly cuisine," it's hard to see the humor in these little medical recants.

For example, having been so thoroughly warned about the dangers of ingesting caffeine, we stoically and collectively stumbled and snored our way through hundreds of mornings, sacrificing our beloved real coffee for blah, unleaded substitutes. About the time we were all falling asleep on our lunch trays, the scientists announced (I imagine with dastardly glee), "Whoops—another boo-boo! Now we have found that the chemicals used to dissolve the caffeine are far more dangerous than drinking the real java. And by the way, a new study shows that one of the ten things centenarians have in common is that they all drank caffeinated coffee. And, we've found—surprise, surprise—coffee actually makes you more attentive. Isn't this amusing?" Garfield the Cat spoke up for the nation when he showed up on a poster, wild-eyed and yelling, "Give me COFFEE now—and no one will get hurt!"

These days strong coffee is not only back in favor, it comes in every flavor—the hip-happenin' beverage of the hour. I think the explosive popularity of Starbucks and other gourmet coffee shops may be the consumers' way of expressing our sheer gratitude for the return of the bean with caffeine. As long lines form behind foaming, spitting cappuccino machines, it's as though we're all paying silent homage. *How we missed you, oh Morning Cup of Fresh Brew! Welcome to our world again, Fresh Ground Hazelnut Beans. Never again will we take you for granted—see, you're practically royalty now.*

Still, the nutrition community persists in its efforts to spoil the joy of most well-loved comfort foods. The mere thought of a warm mug of cocoa or hot apple pie à la mode or french-fried onion rings makes us salivate. Until, that is, we hear doctors warn about the results on our hips and hearts. It's a national, nutritional bummer!

There is, however, a grassroots revolt springing up that will be interesting to watch in coming years. In her book, *Clicking,* famed trend watcher Faith Popcorn points to a new phenomena she coins "Pleasure Revenge." Already "fat-free" products are shown to be sliding off America's grocery lists. "Give us back real cream! Butter! Potatoes fried in oil!" cry the fat-starved masses. Why? According to the *Popcorn Report,* people have been depriving themselves of fat-laden goodies for several years and have not found their lives, on a whole, to be any more fulfilling. (Or "full-feeling" for that matter.) You mean living fat-free was not the big key to perpetual bliss? Ah, well . . . back to the grocery shelf.

Thankfully, there seems to be some good news on this score for those of us who cherish our comfort cuisine and are trying to make peace with our bulging battles. Medical doctor David Sobel, along with his research partner, psychologist Robert Ornstein, asks, "Is being thin worth the daily torture of deprivation, calorie counting, and rigid exercise regimens that it takes for most of us to maintain our 'ideal weight'?" "Probably not," they write. "In fact, being pleasingly plump is healthier than subjecting ourselves to the ups and downs of constant dieting. And while there is no question that what and how we eat is related to our health, 'dieting is not a healthy way to eat.' " *Yes!* I want to shout. *Pleasingly Plumps of the world unite!* (Shall we celebrate by going out for cheesecake and real coffee?)

Leo Buscaglia is a speaker whose outlook on life I've often admired. I think it is because he's the epitome of a big-hearted Italian. (Somehow, I can't help but believe there was a passionate Italian serenading somewhere in my ancestor's genes.) In his book, *Bus 9 to Paradise,* Buscaglia bemoaned the medical assault on his cherished family dishes such as "carbonara with proscuitto, butter and cheese." Leo's mother, noting his distress, gave him some simple advice: "Have it all, Leo, but in moderation." Buscaglia's mother lived a happy life until the ripe, old age of eighty-two. "Not bad for a woman with high blood pressure and astronomical levels of cholesterol," he wrote.

What about all the thin people who sound so well-meaning when they tell their fluffier friends, "I only want you to lose weight for your own self-esteem. It will give you a brighter outlook on life." *"Au, contraire,"* the well-rounded may now answer back with confidence, holding both chins high. Doctors Sobel and Ornstein also say that in spite of popular opinion, "fat people do not seem to have any greater psychological problems than do slim people. Some studies support a 'jolly-fat connection,' in which overweight people show significantly *less anxiety and depression* than do their slimmer peers." Ho-ho-ho! Take that, smug speedy-metabolizers!

Just as I enjoy the variety of foods God has given us, I also love the variety and creativity He used in peopling our planet. Short and tall, plump and skinny, all shades of skin colors, curly and straight hair. Blue, green, brown eyes—big dark round ones from India, tiny slits from the Orient. He even playfully decorated some of us with dimples and chocolate-sprinkle freckles. He gifted us with affectionate Down's Syndrome kids and brilliant Einsteins; Olympic athletes and inspiring paraplegics like Joni Eareckson

Tada. If there's one thing I will mount a soapbox against it is the idea that there is one "ideal" we must all be, or achieve, to be worthy of acceptance. People, like life, need variety to give us spice.

*Bless the L*ORD*. . . . Who satisfieth thy mouth with good things; so that thy youth is renewed like the eagle's.*
(Ps. 103:2, 5, KJV)

chapter twenty-six
GETTING WELL WITH FISH FOOD?

Since finally coming to accept and appreciate the middle-aged body I've been given by my Creator, my focus, in recent months, has shifted from overemphasis on outward appearances to seeking simple ways to keep my body healthy and feeling good. I really *hate* being sick, and last year I had a whole series of months when I could not seem to get well.

I grew weary of seeing doctors, who would order yet one more round of antibiotics that would kill the infection, but the "bug zapper" would also murder some of the good bacteria in my system, setting up the need for yet another round of countermedication. It was a never-ending cycle, with stronger and stronger antibiotics being prescribed each time.

In desperation, I stopped into a health food store one day, poured out my health troubles, and asked the owner if she had any suggestions.

I would find the solution to my health problem in a most unlikely place: at the bottom of a pond.

She smiled and said, "It's really not complicated. Eat a variety of foods you like, especially fresh fruits and vegetables, and enjoy every bite—in moderation." (The wisdom of an Italian mamma echoed across the health food counter.) Her classic "eat-your-vegetables" advice reminded me of a quote I'd clipped from the *Dallas Morning News*. A doctor of thirty-three years and author of *The Doctor Generic Will See You Now* says, "I must admit, the vegetarians whom I treat have the lowest cholesterols, the fewest cancers, the smuggest expressions and the greatest amounts of intestinal gas of any patients in my practice." *I wish I liked to eat veggies better,* I moaned silently. *These days I only* feel *like a vegetable.*

"There is one more thing," the health lady continued. "Our soil has become so depleted of minerals over the years that I would suggest adding some densely packed 'supergreen' food supplements to your diet. Today it takes seventy-five bowls of spinach just to equal the same amount of iron one bowl contained in 1948. One Senate document showed that 99 percent of Americans are deficient in minerals."

I thought about the wisdom and mercy of God in providing for a period of Jubilee for the ground—of letting the soil take time off to replenish itself. *Lord, what have we done to the earth—and our health—in the name of progress?* The owner of the store broke my silent musing when she said, "My mom just had radiation treatments for cancer, so I began feeding her a daily 'green cocktail' of barley grasses and algae. The doctors are amazed by her progress and the lack of severe side effects."

That did it. I walked out of the health food store with my prize in hand: a large jar of spirulina, a blue-green algae compressed into pills. Algae, I discovered as I researched with rising interest, is known as the most nutritious food on the planet. It has properties of both a plant and an animal cell, making it rich in nearly every known vitamin and mineral and amino acids (which make up protein molecules). Since it's an easily digestible food, it's 98 percent assimilable. In other words, your body gets to keep the algae it eats, whereas much of the vitamin and mineral supplements we swallow and the animal protein we eat literally goes to waste.

I began taking four 500 mg tablets right away, and that's the dosage I continue to take to this day. Some people take as a little as 250 mg, some as many as 10 grams, depending on how much energy they need. I usually swallow my "pond food" in the morning on a full or empty stomach, it makes no difference. After all, it's just like eating a bowl of packed-down spinach. (Only it's easier to face a few tablets at this hour of the day than a bowl full of greens.)

Almost immediately I noticed I had more energy, especially in the late afternoon when I would routinely make my bleary-eyed stagger for a bed or couch. Now, if I have time for a nap and I'm tired, I enjoy it thoroughly. (As I've stated, I have a great affection for nap time.) But it's nice to have enough energy to keep going when I can't slow down and stop. Even better, nearly all of my health problems disappeared. For me, this has been the simplest way to stay well that I've ever happened upon. I can forget which vitamins I am supposed to combine with what: It's so much simpler for me to just swallow a whole, vitamin-and-mineral-packed food and be done with it.

Scott, who once thought I was crazy for bringing home edible "green pond food," is now a regular Jolly Green Gent, though he prefers to drink his greens. Every morning he takes a spoonful of "supergreen" powder (also purchased at the health food store)—made from barley, wheat grass, ehlorella (another chlorophyll-rich algae), brown rice, and kelp (yum, yum)—stirs it into a glass of orange juice, and downs it with a satisfied, "Ahhhh." Just the dark green color of it makes the rest of the family gag, but Scott swears it has made all the difference in how he feels and says he can't taste the powder when it's dissolved in juice.

Keep in mind, neither Scott nor I are what you could even remotely call "health nuts." But we've happened upon something our bodies must have been missing, and it's worked so well for us that I want to share it with others just in case it might be of some help. We've not had as much as a cough or cold—even when everyone around us was succumbing to the flu and viruses. All of my infections have cleared up—including the mouth sores—and I have had no recurrences. (Unless I forget to take the spirulina for a couple of days; then my canker sores might begin flaring up again. I just double up taking algae, and the sores heal in a day or so. A painful process that used to take one to two weeks.)

More and more, as the cost of health care soars, we're taking preventive nutrition seriously. Many of you have probably already happened upon some kind of healthy regimen that seems to make a difference in how you feel. Leave it to me to develop an affinity for pond scum. But think about it: God designed algae to grow so easily and abundantly—in both fresh and salt waters—that I can't help but wonder if it was originally created to be a food staple or some sort of supplement for humans and animals. According to experts, there's enough algae right now, waiting to be harvested, to feed the entire world several grams every day. Since it reproduces in mere *hours*—it is a never-ending food source.

I was amazed to discover that spirulina has been approved

in Russia as a "medicine food" for treating radiation sickness. One of the most encouraging reports I read said, "The children of Chernobyl suffer radiation poisoning from eating food grown on radioactive soil. Their bone marrow is damaged, rendering them immunodeficent and unable to produce normal red or white blood cells. They are anemic and suffer from terrible allergic reactions. Children fed just five grams of spirulina tablets each day make dramatic recoveries within six weeks. Children not given spirulina remain ill."

There's even more exciting breakthroughs on the horizon. In April 1996, scientists from Harvard, Dana-Farber Cancer Institute, and other medical institutions announced ongoing research. They found that an extract from spirulina so strengthened the immune system that an extract of it has slowed and even stopped the reproduction of many viruses—including HIV, the AIDS virus. Even at concentrations high enough to destroy a virus, this spirulina formula was found nontoxic to human cells.

One algae packing company out of Klamath Falls, Oregon, donates 10 percent of their product to impoverished children and elderly in Nicaragua, Cambodia, the Dominican Republic, and Guatemala. Not only did the childrens' physical conditions improve dramatically, average test scores at one school rose from 64 percent to 85 percent—after just two months of taking algae.

Again, I'm not a scientist, but this sure seems like exciting and important news packed with hope for the sick, the dying, and the poor in our world—the people Christ tells us to care for.

But back to our own backyard swings. As I was writing this, I happened upon an article on the Internet called "Keep It Simple Sweetheart—with Green Superfoods!" by Barbara Duran. And to me, that's what makes this stuff unique: It is so simple. So for those of you who might want to give "eating green" a shot, here's some information that might be of interest:

GETTING WELL WITH FISH FOOD?

According to the article, there are two types of blue-green algae being sold in the U.S. One is a *wild* blue-green algae, harvested from mineral-rich Klamath Lake in Oregon. It is similar to spirulina but is usually more expensive and is often sold via network marketing—both negatives for many people. Spirulina is harvested and fed from man-made ponds. The good news is that Scott and I have tried both kinds and found the spirulina from the health food store worked as well, if not better, for us. Chlorella is a pure green algae, also packed with nutrition. According to Duran, "Some people find that they digest them better or benefit more when they take the two types of algae (green and blue-green) together."

Ms. Duran ends her article by saying, "While I'm setting my microwave tonight, I will wonder about how protected I am from the invisible waves emanating from this wondrous machine. I suppose I should also wonder about the monitor I sit in front of as this article is being written. I surf the Internet for answers to dietary problems and am given the world's information. There's a lot of it. It's very complicated. It's very stressful. . . .

"I just want some onion rings and ketchup (my vegetables for today) and keep getting my work done. . . . I thank God for some of the simple things in life, and reach for the Spirulina and a jar of wheat and barley grass."

To sum up my personal down-home, back-porch, food-simplifying remedy: Go ahead and have your occasional fried "Bloomin' Onion"! Dig heartily into your apple pie à la mode. Sip hot chocolate on your swing till the sun goes down. All in moderation. Just make sure that you get a nice order of pond food and wheat grass on the side. What could be simpler? Someday, I may even write a children's book about the virtues of pond food. I thought I might title it *Green Algae and Ham* (with apologies to Dr. Seuss).

Would you like green food with ham?

Eat some pond scum, Sam-I-Am!

Would you eat it in a pill? Would you drink it when you're ill?

Would you sip it on a swing? Would you try it in the spring?

Try it, try it, you will see—a green and healthy Jubilee!

To . . . everything that has the breath of life in it—I give every green plant for food.
(Gen. 1:30)

chapter twenty-seven
DIGGING AND PRAYING FOR HEALTH

If we believe everything we read in the newspapers these days, we are a nation of really sick people. As a matter of fact, we have more infirm and afflicted than we have actual citizens. Columnist Bob Garfield recently added up all the millions of people who are supposed to be suffering from sickness (including 12 million Americans who suffer from "restless leg syndrome") and found that the total comes to 543 million disease-ridden Americans "which means—in a country of 266 million people—either we as a society are doomed or someone is seriously double dipping."

Even allowing for errors in addition, there are enough sick people around to make one feel queasy. What's the cure for all that ails us? Since I'm in charge of writing this book, I get to pick and choose to discuss the remedies that most strike my fancy. (Give me an inch. . . .) I've already discussed my diet and pond scum supplement routine. Next, I'd like to talk about exercise.

I love talking about exercise—it is actually doing it that I find so distasteful. Unless I'm getting "by the way" exercise. I love walking, for example, if I'm also shopping for bargains at the big, outdoor market we East Texans know as First Monday. I enjoy calisthenics—when I'm doing deep knee bends and arm reaches while I'm in the process of trying on clothes in a department store dressing room. I don't mind aerobic dancing as long as I can do it while I'm sweeping and mopping the floor. But I do not have the time or inclination to drive thirty minutes in traffic, go to an exercise class for an hour, subject my leotard-lined body to public display just to let all that good energy out into thin air. By the time I drive back home I'm too tired to clean house or go shopping.

One day I met a woman I'd seen once before but she looked much slimmer and more fit than when last we'd bumped into each other. "Wow!" I told her. "You look great! What have you been doing?" Her reply took me off guard. "Digging a fishpond."

"Come again?" I asked.

"Well, I decided one day that I wanted a fishpond in my backyard. So I set out to dig one myself. By the time I'd dug the hole, laid the concrete, set the stones, filled it with goldfish and water, and planted flowers around the edge, I got on the scales, and I'd lost twenty pounds!"

"This is too good," I commented. "You know, together we could start the next health craze—The Fishpond Diet and Exercise Routine."

"Isn't it hilarious?" she giggled.

"I think it's great!" I responded enthusiastically. Then I began to wonder if there were some creative ways I could double up— you know, get fit and get something accomplished at the same time. I uncovered some interesting facts:

DIGGING AND PRAYING FOR HEALTH

A 120-pound woman (for those of you who are lucky enough to be one of them) burns

- 3 calories per minute making the bed or raking leaves (more than bowling or walking at 2 miles per hour)
- 3.5 calories per minute mopping (more than golf or riding horseback)
- 4 calories per minute playing with children and scrubbing walls (same as playing tennis doubles)
- 4.2 calories per minute mowing the lawn (only slightly less than playing half-court basketball)

If you weed and dig in the garden, climb stairs, or like to dance to the radio—you'll burn up as many calories as backpacking, canoeing, skating, or chopping wood.

The houses we live in are virtual gyms. This two-story dweller is *really* living in a gym. Scott, at this writing, is turning our stairwell into a rock climbing gym. I keep whining about the idea, but he keeps saying how I'll love it, how attractive it will be, what great fun it will be for me and the kids. I'll let you know in the next book I write: *My Family Is Climbing the Walls.*

That's all the talk about exercise I can handle right now. I'm already feeling winded from the exertion.

Now here's my favorite health tip, perhaps the most effective of all: prayer. There have been several breakthrough studies in recent years showing that prayer makes a positive difference in recovering health—*even when the sick people don't know that prayer is being made on their behalf.* All other things being equal, a regular churchgoer, statistically speaking, will live longer than someone who has no regular place of worship. Believing is even better for you than was once thought, and the medical profession is finally beginning to take note—and kneel. Dr. Kenneth Cooper, the "father of aerobics," has recently written an entire book on the subject of how belief affects our bodies. Other prominent M.D.'s are following suit.

When my children were small and their heads ached or they had nightmares, inevitably they'd crawl up in my lap and ask me to pray for them. (And when my head ached, I'd put my head in their tiny laps and ask them to do the same for me.) I do not know how I would have survived their childhood illnesses without the soothing resource of prayer. (I'll never forget when the four of them had chicken pox one after another. I don't think I saw the light of day for two months!)

Once I began praying, their little bodies would relax and, almost always, they'd feel better. I have many memories of my mother and father praying aloud at my bedside when I was sick. I never questioned whether or not it would work; I simply relaxed, knowing my body would heal in God's time and that I was loved and cared for until then. To this day, I know the prayers of four believing grandparents make a difference in my children's lives. How comforting to know that heaven is daily bombarded with prayers for our family, that our lives—in sickness and in health—are in His loving hands.

Now if you'll excuse me, I have to go do my laundry aerobics while I pray for my family at the same time. Hey! I just thought of another book I could add to my "health line." I could call it—are you ready for this?—*Pray 'n' Wash!*

(I know. Baaaaaad joke)

Is any one of you sick? . . . pray for each other so that you may be healed. The prayer of a righteous man is powerful and effective.
(James 5:14a, 16b)

chapter twenty-eight
LISTENING WITH YOUR HEART

It is a rare and precious evening. My husband, Scott, and I are curled up on an overstuffed love seat, our legs outstretched and intertwined together on the giant ottoman in front of us. He's drinking a mug of hot, black coffee; I'm sipping herbal tea from a china cup. In the background, romantic music from the 1940s is playing: "Sentimental Journey," "You Made Me Love You." The room is softly illuminated by the light of a lamp and a glowing fire in the hearth.

After traveling all day and speaking to a gathering of bankers' wives, my feelings tonight are a mixture of gratitude, relief, exhaustion, and satisfaction. Ruby Kathryn, the benevolent woman who organized the day's event has seen to it that our time here in

Mississippi includes plenty of southern-style pampering. Knowing Scott was accompanying me, she arranged for our stay in this charming bed-and-breakfast. She even sent a dozen red roses and a gargantuan basket of goodies to our room. Tonight I feel like saluting the South, its charm, and all its Ruby Kathryns.

Not only is this evening special because of the romantic setting away from home, kids, and the phone; it is unusual because I'm not in the mood for talking. I've talked nonstop all afternoon and for now, anyway, have grown weary of the sound of my own voice. I'm in a curious frame of mind—I'm in the mood for *listening*. For a few moments there's silence between us, except for Nat King Cole's crooning, the crackle of burning logs, and an occasional sigh of contentment.

Then something remarkable happens. I ask my husband a couple of questions. Then I focus on his face, listening attentively to his answers. Allowing Scott all the time he needs, I do not interrupt or interject my own thoughts, as is so often my habit. Oh, occasionally I throw in a piggyback question or encouraging comment, but mostly I gently bat the conversational ball back into his court. Amazing. Like a bud opening to flower, I sit in this cozy atmosphere and observe my husband come to life.

My reserved husband is smiling as he chats away the hour. One might even say he is *animated* as he pours out several dreams, plans, and ideas he's been mulling over for months. He is relating on a deeper level than he has in a long, long time. I realize how happy he seems at this moment—how starved he's probably been for the listening ear of a wife who, of late, has been far too preoccupied with herself.

I also realize another truth: Men probably don't stop talking because they aren't "talkers" by nature; they stop talking because we stop *really listening*. They stop talking because when they do talk we criticize them or tease them about their subject choice, judge them, or interrupt them with our views. How long has it been since I've simply listened, with sincere attentiveness, to my husband? How long has it been since I let go of my own agenda and was there for *him*—encouraging and complimenting his terrific thoughts and ideas?

* * *

I'm home again in Texas now, still pondering the gentle art of listening. (And how I really ought to practice it more often.) Apparently this is one of those messages Someone thinks I need to learn, for I had an incredible experience this morning that drove the point home once more.

I meet for breakfast regularly with several gals from my church; this morning we gathered at a local restaurant for breakfast. As in any group there are those of us who excel in talking and attention-getting and others who put up with those of us who excel in talking and attention-getting. My friend, Marilyn, mostly falls into the latter group. She's a quiet one, and the most faithful of friends, but mostly she does lots of listening and affirming. But just when we're lulled into thinking soft-spoken Marilyn is a consistent, not-much-going-on kind of woman, she goes and surprises the whole lot of us.

There was the week, two years ago, when one of us finally stopped talking long enough to ask Marilyn what she'd been up to. Rather nonchalantly she replied, "Well, I just brought home a harp."

"A *what?*" we all asked simultaneously.

"Yes, well, I've always wanted to play the harp, you see, and I decided this week that it's never too late to learn. So I'm taking harp lessons."

Making good on her dream, Marilyn recently wheeled her giant harp through the parking lot and delighted our ladies' church group with heavenly background music.

Then there was the day after we'd all been chatting nonstop when I made a point to ask quiet, calm Marilyn what she had done over the weekend.

"Oh," she said matter-of-factly, "the family flew up to Boston to watch my husband run the Boston Marathon."

"What?"

"Yes, Bob's a runner. Didn't I tell you?"

"Everyone who puts on tennis shoes and jogs around the block says they're a runner, Marilyn," I explained, "but not everyone runs in the Boston Marathon!"

"Oh," she replied thoughtfully. "Well, Bob did. This weekend."

Ay-yi-yi! I thought to myself. *If I'd just come from watching my husband run in the Boston Marathon, I'd have come to lunch today, stood on my chair, tapped my glass with my spoon until I was sure I had everyone's attention, and then loudly made the announcement. I just don't get it. How does she keep news like this from exploding out of her mouth when she first sits down at the table?*

But the harp and the marathon were *nothing* compared to this morning's unassuming announcement. As a matter of fact, this morning everyone else had already left the table to go on about their day when Marilyn cleared her throat and said, "There *is* something I'd kind of like to tell you about, Becky."

"Oh, Marilyn," I said, "I'm so sorry. We were all so busy talking this morning you didn't a chance to get a word in edgewise. What's going on?"

"Well, we got a call this week from Ronald Reagan's personal secretary in response to a letter Bob wrote to the ex-president. She said it was such a nice letter that Mr. Reagan would like to meet Bob and me in person. So we are flying out to California in two days. To meet the president."

"You're kidding, right?"

"No, I'm not."

"Marilyn, this is *unbelievable!!!* You are going to meet Ronald Reagan—the *real Ronald Reagan*—in two days? And you sat all through breakfast with that kind of information stuffed inside you? While you sipped coffee and listened to us drone on about car pools and chicken recipes?!"

"Well, I think what you all have to say is interesting. It's just that I happened to have this lovely thing happen, and I wanted to share it with you but the right pause never came up."

"Marilyn, I promise you—never again will I ever go through any sort of meeting with you without asking you very specifically and pointedly if you have anything on your mind you might like to share with the group!"

Marilyn laughed, and I knew it meant so much to her simply to be heard and acknowledged. Just because someone is quiet by nature does not mean they aren't longing to take part in conversation too. I am determined to be more sensitive in this area. I want to relax the nagging feeling that I'm responsible for the conversational floor show, to shut my mouth and open my ears and heart to others' lives. Dr. Robert Fisher wrote a powerful little book called *Quick to Listen, Slow to Speak*. In it he described being on a long car ride with a man he'd never met before. Fisher wrote, "To my surprise, as I paid close attention to what he was saying, I found myself genuinely interested and involved in the conversation. Occasionally I would make a comment or ask a pertinent question, but I was never asked and never gave any information about myself." At the end of the long ride, the companion said to Dr. Fisher, "I know you're young, but I want you to know you are absolutely one of the finest conversationalists I have ever met." Isn't it interesting? The thing many of us need to learn about being a great conversationalist is to be more active in our listening.

I can count on one hand, maybe two, the people in my life who have gifted me with complete and focused attention, who act as if they have nothing better or more exciting to do than to listen to me and to try to understand the way I think and feel about life or doughnuts or whatever. They leave me feeling so— *affirmed.*

My mother does this beautifully. My husband, bless his heart, listens more than his fair share in our relationship. And as I pointed out, I have a sprinkling of friends I hold especially dear, probably because they make me feel supremely loved by simply listening to me attentively and with compassion. I wholeheartedly agree with Dr. Fisher's comment, "Rapt and exclusive attention is one of the greatest gifts we can give another individual. It is the highest form of compliment."

Is there someone you'd really love to encourage? How about inviting them to your porch swing and blessing them with an unhurried afternoon of focused listening? My therapist friends tell me they'd probably be out of business if enough of us took the time to do this for each other. Taylor Caldwell, in the novel *The Listener,* wrote, "[Man's] real need, his most terrible need, is for someone to listen to him, not as 'patient' but as human soul."

"When someone deeply listens to you," wrote poet John Fox, "it is like holding out a dented cup you've had since childhood and watching it fill up with cold, fresh water. When it balances on top of the brim, you are understood. When it overflows and touches your skin, you are loved." I must admit it is a challenge for us women of the "verbal variety" to listen fully, deeply, and actively to others. But, oh, the rewards of watching their cups fill up with love.

My dear brothers, take note of this: Everyone should be quick to listen, slow to speak.
(James 1:19)

chapter twenty-nine
LOVING IN THE LITTLE THINGS

I've found her! I've finally found her!

Who?

I've found the woman I want to be—the woman who lives in my head but has not, as yet, found her way into my real life. But that's OK. Sometimes these things take time. The woman I want to be is well beyond eighty years old anyway, so I'm thinking perhaps it probably takes a long time to grow a balanced life. My new heroine is an artist. She wears long, antique cotton dresses (with aprons) and bonnets, is barefoot, and has twinkling eyes and a childlike, joyous, mischievous outlook on life. Her name is Tasha Tudor.

I've come to know Tasha Tudor only recently, but many of you may have already discovered this delightful treat of a lady through her dozens of illustrated childrens' books or in one of the beautifully photographed volumes about her life such as *Tasha Tudor's Garden*.

This Christmas, our family was on the receiving end of an unexpected and generous gift from my new friend Ruby Kathryn: three enormous boxes of new books. There were children's books, novels, devotionals, classics, dozens of scrumptious hardback reads, and among all the treasures were the books about Tasha Tudor. For days after opening those boxes I was like a child let loose in a candy store, sampling bites of this book and nibbles of that—anxious to see if the filling tasted as good as the coating advertised. All the books were delightful, but thus far, the Tasha books are my favorites.

When I telephoned to thank Ruby Kathryn and commented on the books I liked best, she replied, "Oh, Becky. I knew you'd love Tasha Tudor's books. Whenever I'm feeling frazzled and frantic I leaf through the beautiful pictures and relaxing words, and like osmosis I absorb it all and find myself feeling calmed again."

During a recent visit with my little sister, Rachel, I asked if she'd ever heard of Tasha Tudor.

"Yes!" Rachel almost shouted, grabbing my arm in a gesture of excitement. "I have an interview with her on video that I'll have to send you. She's the cutest little thing. Sort of an ancient-looking, birdlike woman with a disarming sense of humor. Even her voice is adorable. To her, even the littlest things are 'fun,' 'quite entertaining,' or 'delightful.' She even made being old sound like the best possible stage of life. I remember at one point the camera focused on Tasha as she sweetly painted away on her canvas, talking about how she always draws from real life—instead of pictures. Then she said, 'I have a whole freezer full of little mice that I found in various places, wrapped in death. Would you like to see them?' It was hilarious to imagine this sweet, gentle lady thawing and refreezing an entire morgue of woodland creatures to use as models for her book illustrations!"

"Do you think she's sort of eccentric then?"

"Yes, but in a really delightful, sane sort of way."

"Send me the video—I can always use one more happy, eccentric role model in my life."

My sister's package with the video arrived last week. Appropriately titled, *Take Joy!* I've already watched it over five times, and still, I'm not tired of it. There is so much about this woman that fascinates me. I'm not even completely sure of all the reasons. I certainly don't agree with some of her peculiar ideas about religion (she and her family made one up to their own liking, mostly as an excuse to have a feast and celebrate), but I wholeheartedly embrace her enthusiasm for the simple joys of life.

Tasha loves children, and it is obvious that her own enchanting childhood is never far from her memory. She also loves animals (she has her milking goats, her beloved corgis, and a pet parrot who likes to play dead on the dinner plates); adores her lush flower and herb garden ("I haven't any modesty when it comes to my garden," she says, "I'll boast like mad"); and a great affection for tiny things—dollhouses, miniature furnishings, and the like.

When her children were small, Tasha went to elaborate means to give them fun, happy memories. For example, her children had miniature mailboxes on their bedroom doors. During the day while they were at school, Tasha made the teeniest letters and tiny hand-decorated cards (no bigger than an inch-and-a-half square) and slipped them into the mailboxes, telling her children they were from the doll family. They called this make-believe game "The Sparrow Post." Tasha even made a tiny catalog so the children could order doll dresses and hats from it, paying for their orders with buttons. In a few weeks, the real clothes would arrive— her children never guessing that their mother was the seamstress.

Tasha contentedly admits to having accomplished one of the

things most important to her: She gave her children blissful memories of their childhood. To this day she continues to make marionette puppets, write elaborate plays, and direct her children and grandchildren as they put on productions for the community. I found myself, as I listened and watched, wistfully wishing I could have been part of Tasha's family. Not that I'd trade my own parents for anything, but for pure fun, it appears that having Tasha for a mother might have been better even than having Mary Poppins for a nanny and Pippi Longstocking for a next-door neighbor.

Contemplating this caused me to pause and ask myself a difficult question. "What sort of memories will my own children have of their childhood and, in particular, of their mother?" I wasn't sure, so I sought out my youngest son.

"What will I remember most?" Gabe asked, repeating my question as we drove along in the car, picking up and delivering various siblings from play practice, basketball, and youth group activities. "I'll tell you what I remember: laughing and laughing. In the car. You're always saying the funniest things or laughing at something we said or running over a curb. Yep. I'll remember watching the back ends of cars in front of us, and laughing, and telling you what I want to order at the drive-thru." Hmmm . . . not too shabby a memory, all things considered.

Later that evening, Rachel and her friend Michelle (whom I refer to as "my other daughter") came into my bedroom and found me wrapped in an afghan, like a baby papoose, trying to get warm. (I'm always cold these days, even when everyone else in the house is perspiring. Bring on those midlife hot flashes!) Throwing their lithe, teenage bodies haphazardly on the bed beside me, the girls snuggled their respective chins in the palms of their hands and began chatting in unison about boys and makeup and who said what to whom and did I think this shirt looked good with these jeans or would it go better with the other pair. There was a

short pause as they drew in for breath. Michelle hurried to fill the
silence first.

"Becky," she said, lazily stretching her hands above her head.
"I love talking to you."

"You do?" I asked, encouraged.

"Yeah."

"Why?"

" 'Cause you're so cute! And you make me laugh."

"Yeah," Rachel added. "You're good for talking to. You aren't
much of a housecleaner or cook, but you're fun to be with. When
you aren't having PMS."

"Oh!" added Michelle, turning to Rachel. "Do you remember
that time your mom got so mad at us for making a mess in the living room that she locked us out of the house and threw all the
clothes we'd left in the floor outside? We were standing outside
and all of a sudden shirts, underwear, pants, and towels came flying out the door like laundry ammunition or something."

"Yeah, and I remember it getting kind of cold outside, so we
hurried around putting on all the stuff she threw at us."

I shook my head, remembering the ridiculous rages I've occasionally unleashed on my kids—especially when hormones took
their monthly dip—wishing I had a magic eraser to take away all
the Bad Mother Memories and restock them with a line of pure
Fun Mom ones. My only comfort is that most of my friends wish
they could do the same. Nobody I know in my real life world is a
Tasha Tudor Mother—at least not consistently. Still, it is good for
us to have something lofty to aspire to, to help us remember that
it is the little daily spices we parents throw in, a pinch here and
there, that make the soup of our kids' childhoods delicious or bit-
ter and distasteful.

This afternoon I received a phone call from one of my dearest
friends, Brenda, a fellow writer and licensed family counselor. She

said, "Becky, I'm teaching this parenting class, and it is really interesting. There they are—all fresh-faced and eager, pen and pencil in hand, ready to get this 'parenting thing' down pat, ready for guidelines and maps and enforcing discipline. My first step in the class may surprise them. I'm simply going to remind them that kids are fun and to be enjoyed. As a matter of fact, I'm going to use *Worms in My Tea* as a resource!"

"Brenda," I responded with excitement, "I'm so touched! Or as they say in counseling circles, I feel so *affirmed.*"

I often don't know what I am doing as a parent. Who, in reality, knows exactly how to raise kids? (Except people who don't have any yet.) But I do believe it is the little things that count most. When they were small, I cherished the time I had with my children—time to cuddle, rock, sing, talk, and read. Not that it was always easy, mind you. Four preschoolers were my constant and abiding companions; I don't think I went to the bathroom alone, even once, during the entire decade of the eighties. Now that they are growing up, it seems that we're gathering most of our "mother/child moments" on the run.

So I'm sure my children will have memories of a family in too much of a hurry, but hopefully they'll also remember laughter echoing over idling engines. They may recall a mom who once threw the laundry out the door, but they'll also remember a mom who joined them in tossing bread dough on the ceiling to see if it would stick. (It did.) I pray every day that God will allow them to remember more laughter and dough on the ceiling than yelling and throwing. For I realize all too well it is the little things that go into a child's memory bank (and help determine how long our child may have to sit in a therapist's chair someday to undo our less-than-perfect deposits).

Toward the end of *Take Joy!* the narrator quotes a poem by Evelyn Underhill, one of Tasha's favorites. There is a phrase in that poem I keep running over in my mind as one would a smooth pebble in a pocket.

" 'I come in the little things,' saith the Lord."

I come in the little things. When I think of what I love most about being a child of my heavenly Father, it is the little things I'm most thankful for. While sitting on our dock by the sparkling lake, I made up yet another country-style ditty in response to the beautiful ways God touches my days with little things. (Someday, I plan to put together a whole album called *Becky's Little Ditties by the Dock: Songs to Embarrass Your Children By.*)

You Fill Me Up

Sunlight on the water, reflections of Your grace
My husband's kiss still lingers warm in a spot right here
    on my face
The kids are laughin' and cuttin' it up outside my
    backporch door
Everytime I think I've been given enough, You keep on
    givin' me more.

You fill me up, Lord, You give me so much
Just look at this stuff flowin' over my cup
You fill me up, Lord, You give me so much
All these gifts of love, flowing down from above.

Got around to reading my Bible on the lampstand by my
    bed
Uncovering hidden treasures in Your living Word as I
    read

A View from the Porch Swing

Gems and pearls of wisdom from Solomon to Paul
Every time I think I've been given enough, Your love
    continues to fall.

You fill me up, Lord, You give me so much
Just look at this stuff flowin' over my cup
You fill me up, Lord, You give me so much
Little gifts of love, flowing down from above.

Yes, when He comes to grace my life on the backporch of my soul, it is most often in small ways. In Francis Schaeffer's classic book, *No Little People,* he wrote, "The scripture emphasizes that much can come from little if the little is truly consecrated to God."

May I, too, be aware that it is the *little things,* like droplets of spring rain, that water my family's garden of memories with seeds of love.

Well done . . . because you have been faithful in a very little thing.
(Luke 19:17, NASB)

chapter thirty
WINNING WITH GRACE

Scott, in his matter-of-fact style, once said something profound. (He's probably said something profound more than once, it's just that this one quote stands out.) He said, "Most Christians I know who think they are being persecuted for their faith aren't being persecuted for their faith. They are being persecuted for being obnoxious."

Are some of us trying so hard to be good that we're forgetting to be kind? It's like the young child who prayed, "Oh, God, make all the bad people good, and make all the good people nice." How often are Christians losing our "fight for the right" because we lack a spirit of love in *how* we communicate our views to the world? I see this not only in politics and the church at large, but

I'm ashamed to admit I often see this attitude creeping into my own life. Unfortunately, this is what keeps relationships from experiencing more Jubilees—times of refreshment and forgiveness—when we find a relaxed joy in each other's company.

I've noticed that often it is bright, intelligent people who are most vulnerable to falling into the trap of one-upmanship. You know the type. They seem to be on constant Debate Mode, ready to nail any wrong to the wall in a single, verbal blast. It must be hard for them—they know all the answers, so how can they let untruths slide by undebated? But what and where does it get them? Where is the taste of victory when there's no one to cheer and everyone's pinned to the wall, busy licking their puncture wounds? The old saying is powerfully true: No one cares what you know unless they know that you care.

He who is most gracious wins.

When I allow this truth to sink into my head, my neck muscles relax, my fists unclench, and I realize that even if I am in the right, I will ultimately lose what's really important if I let my desire to win take over my ability to show love.

Our beloved Sunday school teacher, Ed Wichern, never ceases to amaze me. His patient, kind, and gentle ways have endeared him to every person in our class. The thing that really amazes me is that Ed remains ever patient, kind, and gentle with a class filled with some pretty radical, sharp-tongued, and off-the-wall people. (Present company sometimes included.) When someone in the class blurts out something wrong or completely off-base, it is an incredible lesson in human relations to watch Ed at work. He thoughtfully nods in the dissenter's direction, affirming them as a person worthy of love, and generally says something on the order of, "Isn't God good? We don't know all the answers, and yet we can rest in the fact that He loves every one of us in spite of our differing opinions." Then he deftly turns in his Bible to the next verse.

This operation reminds me of a skillful parent, replacing a china cup with a plastic toy—the exchange occurring so swiftly and smoothly that the toddler forgoes his usual tantrum. Ed has expertly diverted more than his share of adult Sunday school fits.

The late Dr. Francis Schaeffer was one of the greatest Christian thinkers of this century. After I used his quote from *No Little People* in this book, I found the latest copy of *Christianity Today* sitting in my mailbox. I was amused by the portrait on the cover with the inscription "Our Saint Francis." It was a well-balanced article that brought back many memories. In reminiscing about Dr. Schaeffer's impact on my family's life, I realized that, to me, what he said was secondary in significance to *how* he said it.

This apologist, philosopher, theologian, historian, and student of art, music, and politics spent his life arguing the logical case for the validity of Christianity in our modern world. And yet, he was amazingly gracious and humble in the midst of debate and discussion—especially in his later years. Gentle eyes peered out of his elflike face. He customarily wore knickers, knee socks, and soft, knit shirts rather than intimidating three-piece suits. When my parents were in their thirties, struggling in their own search for ultimate Truth, they were drawn to Schaeffer's works and eventually spent time studying under his teaching at L'Abri (meaning "the shelter") in the mountain village of Huemoz, Switzerland. Love ruled Francis Schaeffer's words in writing and debate as it did his life.

In the late 1970s Scott and I, along with thousands, attended Schaeffer's breakthrough "How Should We Then Live?" conference in Dallas. My young, collegiate head was pounding with all the information. The brainpower floating around that auditorium was palpable. During a question-and-answer session one afternoon, a particularly obnoxious (and possibly mentally ill) young man took the microphone and blasted an incoherent question toward Schaeffer. *What will Dr. Schaeffer do with this one?* I wondered as I fidgeted around in my chair. *He's really in up to his knickers now.*

In short, the crowded auditorium witnessed love in action. Schaeffer poured the love of God on this confused young man, diffusing him of anger. It was like watching a balloon released of its air. Years of patiently working with people had taught Dr. Schaeffer when it was time for intellectual/theological arguments and when it was time for simply sharing God's love. According to the article in *Christianity Today,* Francis tended to be more sharp-tongued in his early years of ministry. "But in later years, wounds inflicted and received spurred him to serious reflection about how to handle theological disagreement in a spirit of genuine Christian love."

In *Francis A. Schaeffer: Portraits of the Man and His Works,* a close friend of the Schaeffers, Louis Parkhurst, remembered a similar incident with a young man who had come to L'Abri for the sole purpose of challenging Dr. Schaeffer. "Although [the young man] was abusive and continually made dogmatic statements against Christianity, Schaeffer neither lost his refined attitude nor allowed the man to walk over him. Each time he was cut off, Dr. Schaeffer would calmly reply, 'Well, if you would just let me finish my sentence. . . .' only to be cut off again. Unable to blow Dr. Schaeffer's composure, the young man eventually backed off, but with a deep and lasting impression having been made upon him. Some time later the young man remarked that, 'Dr. Schaeffer was the first Christian I could not make angry, who would not lash out or be driven into a corner.' "

I recently read with great interest that Bishop Pike, the priest who became famous for his venture into the world of the occult, was involved in two debates toward the end of his life. The first debate pushed Pike further away from Christianity—in part, because of the opponent's obnoxious attitude. But in the second debate his opponent was Dr. Francis Schaeffer, who touched not only Bishop Pike's mind, but also his heart. On the day Bishop

Pike died, he was making plans to visit Dr. Schaeffer at his mountain home in Switzerland. I don't know who won the debate, but I know who won lasting respect. *He who is most gracious wins.*

Without love, even the soundest of theories are nothing but hollow, meaningless words thrown at others who may go away challenged but untouched and unchanged. Again, I know from hard experience. I've been there—even in my own marriage.

A few years back Scott and I were at an impasse. I'd read all the books and thought I knew all the intellectual answers to our problems (if only Scott would listen!). We both saw a marriage counselor, who provided some help, but still we were stuck in theorizing and arguing in our own defense until we'd exhausted ourselves in the effort of trying. Our debate was at a standstill, both of us fighting for our rights, intensely lonely in the battle. Then, in one afternoon, our marriage began to turn around. The wall between us came crumbling down, not because one of us finally won the great debate, turning the other to our own point of view. It happened because of a most insignificant item: a ham sandwich.

We were on vacation, and I was reading a book on the beach—probably a book on how to have a successful marriage. Suddenly I felt a shadow looming over me, and, shading my eyes, I peered upward. There stood Scott, smiling and holding out a plain, ham sandwich, like a little boy offering a weed to his mother.

White bread, ham, and a few sprinkles of sand.

But just as a weed seems like a prized orchid when it's offered from the hand of a child, the sandwich looked gourmet to me. For I was starving—not just for food, but for the emotional nourishment of feeling cared for by my mate. I swallowed a lump in my throat, thanked my husband for his thoughtfulness, and there we sat together in silence, crunching the meager picnic lunch, sipping Dr. Peppers, and watching blue-green waves lap at the shore.

Later that afternoon, we went back to our room, put down our boxing gloves, left our respective debate platforms, and melted into each other's arms. Months of coldness vanished with the presentation of one sand-sprinkled ham sandwich. That night I wrote the following entry in my notebook:

Ham Sandwich
It was only a simple ham sandwich
But I was hungry—and my husband fed me
I was thirsty—he gave me drink
and deep inside a dam burst and exploded
A simple kindness
To me
For no reason
Why am I so overwhelmed with this gift?

Scott, too, had argued his side of our "problems" for a long time. But I could not hear him until I was emotionally fed, secure of his sincere care and concern for me. Now we were free to start a period of jubilee in our marriage—my ears able to hear all he needed to say. Love, expressed in kindness, permits us to unfold.

Yes, he who is most gracious wins.

Words from a wise man's mouth are gracious.
(Eccles. 10:12)

chapter thirty-one
UNWINDING WITH A KINDRED SPIRIT

I made a friend today—we immediately recognized in each other a kindred spirit. Not that we've ever met. Actually, this is the first time I've ever heard from her. And she lives in Korea, so it's not going to be easy to get together for lunch at McDonald's. Still, we're sure we are sisters to the core. Read and you'll understand.

Dear Becky,

As I was reading *Worms in My Tea,* I found myself thinking, *Aha! A kindred spirit!* This person would be a friend I could laugh and cry with.

Three of my five are boys. We are Baptist missionaries to Korea, and living in a foreign culture creates a whole new scope of parenting challenges. Imagine walking into your kitchen to find an 8-inch octopus slithering across the floor, one tentacle at a time—then watching that same octopus suffer a cruel death when one son decides as a saltwater animal it needs a cupful of table salt dumped into its water bowl.

Then there are those well-meaning ladies at the open market who give our boys a jar full of 4-inch, eel-like fish that refuse to die, even though they sit in the same jar without food or fresh water for 3 months. (That explains why Koreans eat them alive.)

I've opened the bathroom door to find that my sons, naked except for makeshift towel loincloths, have used up my 4-year supply of eye shadow and hair mousse to cover themselves with war paint and sculpt their hair into rock-hard mohawks. "My mousse!" I cry in dismay, to which the youngest replies, "I know what a moose is—it's a camel with horns."

And of course our white, fluffy mutt dog couldn't escape for long. She ended up a beautiful shade of blue, a product of the boys' creative urges.

Even now that they are teenagers, I never know what to expect. And I love it.

During the years I had four preschoolers and my house looked like a new tornado came through daily, I heard more than once that my children needed more discipline, when actually all they needed was a bit less exuberance. However, I wouldn't have changed any part of it. As a matter of fact, I enjoyed it so much that we started again, adopting a Korean baby girl 4 years ago when our big kids were 10, 12, 14, and 16.

See what I mean? I wish our paths had crossed at some time, because you seem to be a person with whom I could share war stories, without your looking shocked and disapproving.

Now I ask you, is there anything more freeing or more relaxing than discovering you are not alone in the world? Vivian and I comfort each other by just knowing that we both exist and function even on separate continents, an ocean away. There have been many times when I've wondered if there could possibly be other "Beckys" out there. I mean, does anybody identify with my peculiarities?

I attend a church made mostly of engineers and their families. The one big business in our small town is a technical industry. Actually I'm not sure what it's about, but it's got lots of huge, windowless buildings, and I hear that airplanes carrying important government officials sometimes fly in and out of the nearby airfield. I'd rather be locked up in a mental institution than work in one of those technical plant places. At least you could count on some interesting activity at a mental facility. Anyway, the point I was going to make is that engineers tend to pick wives that at least somewhat complement their personalities.

They tend to choose women who are somewhat organized and thoughtful, deliberate and sane. An engineer would never, ever, in his wildest computer-graphic dreams marry someone, say, like me. I would drive your average engineer personality type stark raving mad in less time than it would take them to access the 'Net. So most of the local available women friends tend to be quite unlike me. Now if I lived in California or Colorado or somewhere more artsy-craftsy than Greenville, Texas, I probably wouldn't stand out—wearing my favorite hot pink sunglasses and lemon-yellow smiley-face hat—quite so obviously.

Sometimes it is hard not to wonder about myself when I'm constantly bumping up against women who have it all together. Even if I manage, on occasion, to get it all together, there's a greater than 50 percent chance I'll lose it before I get it where it needs to go.

Our ten-year-old son, Gabe, had a bit of a struggle adjusting to his new teacher this year. The first day of school he came home and said, "Mom, she's just way too organized." Bless his heart, I should have warned him that any woman who wears matching socks is more organized than his mother.

I wondered if this year might be a challenge when Gabe's teacher called and asked if she might come over and make a home visit before school even started. I must say I was impressed. Mrs. Bailey showed up precisely on time. She was dressed in immaculate teacher attire—down to the apple appliquéd socks and tiny apple earrings. She even had a business card for us. How did I greet this wonderfully together teacher?

I was running late (have I ever "run on time"?), so I met Mrs. Bailey just as I was exiting the shower. My hair was dripping wet. I had no makeup on. I did have a cotton dress thrown on over my damp body, but no shoes or socks. As fate would have it, Gabe's teacher had come not only to meet us but to take a Polaroid picture of Gabe with his mom and dad in their natural home setting. *Oh well,* I thought to myself as I stood dripping next to my child, *at least Gabe will recognize his mother on the bulletin board of family pictures. She'll be the one on the left side of the picture, most resembling a drowned rat.*

You can imagine, after several scenes such as the one above, after I've spent lots of time with women who carry Day-timers and remember to pick up their children on time, my sense of worth might occasionally waver. In most candid group pictures of me and my friends, I'm always the one with my shirt on inside out, hair mussed, and eyes frantically searching the room for a purse or a missing set of keys.

There's nothing like a kindred spirit to breathe new life into strange bodies. Like Vivian said, I want "a person with whom I could share war stories" without them looking shocked and disapproving. Perhaps even a person that would laugh aloud and shout, "I know just what you mean! I'm the same way!" A person you could invite over for tea, and when you forget to put the water on to boil, they don't mind because they don't remember why they've come over in the first place. A person who understands the logic of not sorting the silverware or making the bed.

A person with whom you could relax on the porch swing of life—even though you both have an odd tendency to trip on the grass and, occasionally, fall out of the swing.

A friend loves at all times.
(Prov. 17:17, NASB)

chapter thirty-two

LETTING GO TO BE FREE

From my back porch one summer morning I watched an object lesson unfold, like some sweet story in a children's book.

The evening before, my children had found a baby blue jay struggling (and failing) to fly from the grass. To save the little foundling from becoming "dog food," they picked it up and brought the tiny creature to me. It opened its wide mouth expectantly. When it didn't get the desired worm right away, it began to chirp. Incessantly. So I mixed up some baby cereal with a little water and tried to feed the poor orphan. The results of our feeding time were similar to what happened when I tried to give my own babies their first spoonful of Pablum. More cereal landed on beak and feathers and the front of my shirt than went down the hungry throat of the baby bird. *There's more to being a mother bird than I bargained for,* I thought.

Finally, exhausted from effort, both the bird and I fell asleep. The next morning I awoke to a sharp series of chirps. "Look, little guy," I said loudly over his chirping, "I'd love to help you more than anything. But I just don't know how. Let's go look for your momma." I took my little noisemaker outside and balanced him carefully on the porch rail. Then I walked back inside the house and watched him from the sliding glass door. "Please, Lord," I prayed, "bring help!" I could hear the pitiful chirps through the glass.

Within a few seconds, the glorious sight of a mother bird flew into view. She coaxed the baby to follow her off the porch and up onto the safety of a nearby limb. "Yes!" I cheered from my observation point. "You can do it. Your mom's here now. Fly!" At that moment I spied a black-and-white cat slinking across the yard, looking exactly like Sylvester the cartoon cat. My heart stopped. My little "Tweety Bird" was a wobbly flyer at best. One false move and he would be breakfast.

Suddenly, a streak of blue plummeted from the sky and attacked the stalking cat. Was it a plane? Was it Superman? No—it was Daddy Bird to the rescue. I laughed in delight as I watched the big blue jay tease and divert the attention of the cat, long enough for Momma Bird to get Baby Bird to a higher perch. I smiled, satisfied with the world, as I watched the family fly off together and "Sylvester" still lickin' his frustrated chops.

Not audibly, but still plainly, I felt God saying to me, "This was My lesson for you today, Becky. You are a 'fixer' by nature. You enjoy the strokes you receive from helping others—from 'saving' them. But guess what? You can't fix everything that goes wrong and everyone that is hurting. Sometimes, all you need to do is *let go.* Stand and watch while I take care of the job. I have plenty of momma and daddy birds in my kingdom who are often more qualified to help than you are. Your 'job' in solving many problems is to simply to let go, watch, and pray."

Catherine Marshall came to a similar place in her spiritual walk when she practiced what she called a prayer of relinquishment. On the morning of September 14, 1943, tired of wrestling and begging God to heal her, she said, "I'm beaten through, God. You decide what You want for me." She went on to say, "Tears flowed. I had no faith as I understood faith, expected nothing. The gift of my sick self was made with no trace of graciousness."

And the result? "It was as if I had touched a button, one that opened windows in heaven; as if some dynamo of heavenly power began flowing, flowing. Within a few hours I had experienced the presence of the Living Christ in a way that wiped away all doubt and revolutionized my life. From that moment my recovery began." Her conclusion was that "God absolutely refuses to violate our free will; that, therefore, unless self-will is voluntarily given up, God cannot move to answer prayer."

Voluntarily giving up? "Letting go." In how many areas could I apply this to my life—and possibly find the peace I've been seeking? I could let go of having to meet everyone's needs. I could let go of the feeling that I'm solely responsible for keeping the house clean and, instead, delegate chores! I could ask for all kinds of help in areas in which I'm not gifted—organization, discernment—and not feel guilty for my shortfall. I could give my children and their future up to God! I could quit trying to figure out how to make the perfect marriage and give it to God instead.

Let's see, I could let go of perfection. I could let go of my need for approval! I once heard a man ask an audience, "What risks would you take? What would you do if you let go of seeking the approval of man?" I let those two questions ring in my head, over and over again, for days. I realized I'd feel truly free, perhaps for the first time in my life, if I began to live for God's approval and gave up my gnawing need for the applause of others. "Do your work heartily, as to the Lord, rather than to men" (Eph. 6:7) has become a daily reminder—a thought to refocus my day. One by one, God seems to be leading me through experiences that teach me to let go of all of my sources of approval—including the approval of my friends, my audiences (both my reading and listening audiences), and finally, perhaps, even the approval of my parents.

Though I dearly love and respect my parents today (even more than ever), I've found new freedom in letting go of needing their "OK" on everything I decide to do or choose to believe.

I could let go of grudges and deep disappointments. Anabel Gilham tells people to do this "letting go" in a visual and memorable way. She suggests taking a helium-filled balloon, an indelible marker, and going off alone to a quiet place, like a park. Write whatever it is you need to let go of—burdens, bitterness, whatever is weighing you down—on the balloon (you may want to use a code between you and God). Then release it to God, let the balloon go, and watch it taken up into the sky until it disappears.

Several years ago, baseball great Mickey Mantle died after a long battle with liver disease—a result of years of alcohol abuse. Before his death, there were several stories circulating that he made his peace with Christ during the last year of his life. His funeral made the front page of the *Dallas Morning News*. I've never been a big fan of baseball, but when I saw the front page picture of a little boy sitting on a curb, head down, wearing a shirt with Mickey's number on it, I was touched. Who wouldn't be?

I scanned the article quickly, but one phrase caught my eye. So much that I put it to memory. The reporter wrote, "And in the end, his fans forgave him for being human." As I take in the view from life's front porch and mentally see the parade of friends and family that have come and visited and gone on their way, I see their faults and fears and failures. I know they also see mine. Yet as long as we're stuck in this place "with skin on" we have a choice to make. Will we hold our "humanity" against ourselves, or will we, in the end, let go of judgment and forgive each other for being human? It doesn't take a genius to figure out which choice brings more peace. But it helps to be reminded by a little boy, sitting on the curb, shedding tears of love for a fallen hero whose feet were made of clay.

The time of Jubilee was a time of healing and celebration for many reasons—but perhaps none were more important than the rituals of "letting go." Slaves and prisoners were set free; debts were forgiven; families once divided were to return back home to unite again as a clan. It was the ultimate "clean slate" experience.

When Jesus made His first public proclamation, revealing who He really was, the moment was both dramatic and palpable. After returning from a time of testing in the desert, Jesus went to His boyhood town of Nazareth. On the Sabbath day, someone handed Him the scroll of the prophet Isaiah. Jesus carefully unrolled the parchment and found the place He wanted to read.

"The Spirit of the Lord is on me, because he has anointed me to preach good news to the poor. He has sent me to proclaim freedom for the prisoners and recovery of sight for the blind, to release the oppressed, to proclaim the year of the Lord's favor."

A hush settled over the synagogue; everyone's eyes were riveted to this powerful, gracious man, Jesus. He began his sermon that morning, after the reading of Scripture, by saying, "Today this scripture is fulfilled in your hearing" (Luke 4:18–21).

What did this mean? And what does it have to do with this book about Jubilee? Everything. *The year of the Lord's favor,* according to Hebrew scholars, is simply another term for the Year of Jubilee. What this means to us is that Jesus came as a ransom to buy back our freedom. As the praise song says, "Jesus is our Jubilee."

He comes to free us—like trapped birds to the heavens—from whatever cages of sin we are in.

That's the simple sum of it. Jesus rescued us, His children, in order to set us free—in every conceivable area of our lives. The greatest of all Jubilees.

Your Father's here. All is well. Let go of the struggle and fly!

"Look at the birds of the air; they do not sow or reap or store away in barns, and yet your heavenly Father feeds them. Are you not much more valuable than they?"
(Matt. 6:26)

_____...More Porch Swing Humor from
Becky Freeman

Still Lickin' the Spoon

In her fourth book, best-selling humorist Becky Freeman reminds us that childlike truths can mirror deeper human emotions. This collection of stories offers a humorous, uplifting view of life that proves even the greatest spiritual truths can tickle your funnybone. Chapter titles are taken from the things we loved to do as kids.   0-8054-6279-1

Marriage 911

With the same unique perspective that produced the best-selling _Worms In My Tea_ and _Adult Children of Fairly Functional Parents_, Becky Freeman turns her wit and warmth to the subject of marriage. Beginning with her thoughts and dreams as a 17-year-old bride, Becky's own married life offers reassuring proof that two people who love each other according to God's teaching can keep pasted together (more or less) in spite of screaming kids, bouncing checks, and PMS.   0-8054-6178-7

Adult Children of Fairly Functional Parents

Fresh from their best-selling book, _Worms In My Tea and Other Mixed Blessings_, this daughter-mother writing team examines the love, laughter, and liability that's all a part of the "Sandwich Generation," those who coexist more-or-less peacefully with children on one hand (or in one room) and parents on (or in) the other.   0-8054-6155-8

Worms In My Tea

This best-seller provides a little comic relief from managing a family and raising children, along with biblical truths about our lifelong walk with God.   0-8054-6143-4

Available at fine Christian bookstores everywhere